FORD
——
NEW YORK
IS NOT
AMERICA

F
128.5
.F7

NEW YORK IS NOT AMERICA

Books by
FORD MADOX FORD

SOME DO NOT . . .
NO MORE PARADES
A MAN COULD STAND UP
A MIRROR TO FRANCE

(To be published)
THE LAST POST

NEW YORK IS NOT AMERICA

BEING A MIRROR TO THE STATES
BY FORD MADOX FORD

*For I love my love for his way of walking,
And I love my love for his way of talking,
And I love my love for his eyes so blue;
If he loved not me what should I do?*

ALBERT & CHARLES BONI

NEW YORK  MCMXXVII

Copyright, 1927, by Albert & Charles Boni, Inc.

Printed in the United States of America

CONTENTS

		PAGE
AUTHOR'S ADVERTISEMENT		vii

CHAPTER
I.	TRAVELERS' TALES	17
II.	MY GOTHAM	41
III.	SKYSCRAPERS	73
IV.	IT IS NOT SO MUCH THE PLACE	100
V.	... AS THE PEOPLE	141
VI.	THE LORDLY DISH	188
VII.	REGIONS CÆSAR NEVER KNEW	215
VIII.	L'ENVOI	288

AUTHOR'S ADVERTISEMENT

I BEG—I beg—I *beg*—the reader of the pages that follow not to imagine that their author is that ludicrous and offensive being, the superior European, or the superior Briton who patronizes American peoples and institutions as if they were children or the products of childish minds. He is, I assure you, this Author, so instinct with the sense of the equality of all human beings—that sense of their equality is to such an extent an instinct with him that he takes all humanity very seriously—and pleasantly. Humbly even, if he does not happen to know them well. For, if he knows them well or, still more, if he is fond of them, he is apt between loving speeches to make fun of them—but if he does not know them well he is apt to be afraid of them. Nay, more, he is dead certain to be afraid of them.

So, loving New York next to Provence, better than any other place, he lets himself go and writes of her as he would talk to his mother or his mistress, being very fond of them. (I am bound to say that at times he will singularly irritate those gentle creatures. But he does not mean to. His heart is in the right place be his tongue never so cheerful.) But knowing nothing at all of America (*What* is America; *who* is the true American?—the Westerner? the Easterner? the Middle Westerner? the Kansan? the Virginia Gentleman? the Harvard Graduate? . . . Answer somebody!) . . . Knowing, then, nothing at all of America except that the New Yorker whom he loves is no American this author is singularly afraid of all America and all Americans. He ventures outside the charmed circle of Gotham with the timorous sensation of one inserting his toe into the sea in order to test its temperature. It is not that he fears the terrible gunmen—for he believes them to be the admirable fairy tales of a press splendidly equipped to entertain its patrons. He himself never saw a gunman nor any one who had ever seen a gunman; he himself has never come across a crime or a trace of crime in the whole United States, except for certain crimes committed, mostly in basements, by himself and confederates. No, it is not even the almost more terrible police, not even the acts of Volstead or Man, that make him afraid of America: it is just the dread of the unknown . . . of the unknown, that is, according to all Americans, the Unknowable. It is the feeling that overwhelms the small child when he stands with fingers on the door of a great drawing-room that is full, full, full of adult and ironic strangers. . . .

So this author, professing to know New York, professes no knowledge at all of America. And he professes to know New York only just as one knows London or Paris—or England or France: one's little patch of each. He knows, that is to say, how to live automatically and at ease, pretty well anywhere between the Battery and the further end of Central Park—without asking for directions or for information as to where to purchase postage stamps or socks or where to dine; he can live there without the remotest feeling of strangeness, perfectly himself. That is perhaps all that the phrase "knowing the city" can be stretched to imply.

You say "So and So knows his Paris" but it is only *his* Paris that he knows—for when it comes to knowledge he does not even know his own soul.

To this sort of ability of living within a city as easily as you can live within your own old clothes you must add affection—for to live in a city and hate it will never give you the right to say that you "know" it ... or to call it "yours."

That right this author claims—the right to write of *"my* Gotham": he *has* his image of the great, easy, tolerant, glamorous place.

You may complain that that image is not yours: that cannot be helped. You did not pay your money—you were certainly not asked to—to read your own deductions from statistics and newspaper columns. You can make those for yourself. This author reads no statistics and very few newspapers—and no books on the subject written by other, informative writers. He moons about the places that he likes, writing usually stuff of some sort or other about subjects quite different. Then he writes the résumé of his mental adventures.

You will say that this is mere autobiography. Well, it is mere autobiography—of an angle of a human being. ... But think how much richer the world would be for the autobiography of such an angle of Shakespeare's being in, say, Denmark, when he was a strolling player; or of Dante at Oxford —or of Chateaubriand in America. So for such books there may be a place.

There is another side to it. This author has spent his life—such portions of it as he has devoted to the public service—in unceasingly pointing out the sameness of humanity in all nations and down all the ages. Here he is at it again. That is the only sane Internationalism. If one-tenth of the sums spent on diplomacy or international leagues were spent on saying: "Here we are; we are just all merely poor humanity making our voyage upon a spinning planet that is whirling to its doom somewhere in space," there would be no more international misunderstandings; for sure there would be no more war.

If a man from, say, Avignon could be got to say to all Chicago, and a man from Chicago to say to all Avignon: "We are exactly the same food for crows. If sudden death should strike down your or my little daughter should we not feel it alike? If smut should destroy our wheat, murrain our beasts, bankruptcy our trades shall we not feel it alike? Have we not the same joys; the same hopes; identical causes for despair? Then in the name of God, why should we bicker? . . . Let our ambassadors be our books. Could you kill a Jew just after reading the lament of Saul for Absalom or an American just after reading *"When lilacs last in the doorway bloomed. . . ."* I do not believe it. . . . If members of nations could be got so to speak to strange nations there would be no need for Geneva.

It is in the hope that a few more souls can be got to share this belief that this author has written this book. If that is accomplished he will have done the state some service.

. . . .

Just before writing the above I had watched the great black, light-pierced hill that towers above the Battery and the North River Piers withdraw little by little. Little roads on the slope were indicated by chains of lamps; high on the left towered the lit windows of a cathedral, ablaze on the black background. . . . One is never certain that one will return . . . not *certain*.

It is not decent to describe for an Anglo-Saxon audience the emotions that one feels at such thoughts as that it is not certain that one will ever return. One day I will do it in French—and be sure that it will be a lament; if it is well done it will be a very soul-searching lament.

The ship, moved and moved, nuzzled and pulled at by tugs as bread on water is beset by small fish. In the river there was a mist of which we were insensible because of the blackness of the February night. The lights became astonishingly fewer; we looked ahead to see what there was where we were heading to. . . . When we looked back there was only blackness: not even the reflection of pier-lamps on the water, so little power have electric rays to pierce mist. There was no more Gotham.

Off Nantucket, 24th Feb., 1927.

To JEANNE M. FOSTER

MY DEAR JEANNE:

Here I am back after all, just in time to dedicate this New York edition to the kindest of New Yorkers.

Yours gratefully and with affection,

F. M. F.

New York, Oct. 25th, 1927.

NEW YORK IS NOT AMERICA

NEW YORK IS NOT AMERICA

CHAPTER I

TRAVELERS' TALES

A YEAR or so ago when I was coming over here on the *Paris* there was a great storm. There was so great a storm that only fifteen of us attended breakfast. In consequence, there seated herself beside me a lady of a certain age whom I had not before noticed. She remarked to me suddenly—this sort of thing happens only to travelers—she remarked to me, then, suddenly with an organ more singularly nasal than any I have hitherto had the good fortune to encounter:

"You kehn't flirt with Amur'can gels as you ken with English ones. But if she falls in love with you . . . *look aout.*"

That was all she said, and it is all that I can remember of her, save that she was large, florid, and alarming. And the assault was so unprovoked—for there certainly wasn't any she to whom the message could apply—it was all so singular in that reeling ship that she remains to me as something supernatural. If there were here any female figure equivalent to that of our Britannia on the pennies, and if the voice had not been so singularly nasal that the suspicion would be insulting, I should have imagined that the Genius of the land which we were approaching had manifested itself, and that She—right or wrong—felt sufficiently interested in my unworthy self to afford me that warning.

Anyhow, it warned me. For the whole of that visit I walked the streets with my eyes glued to the pavement, for, had I chanced to have had handed to me, as we say, a glad eye, how mightn't I have had to look out!

I was going somewhat later on the train to somewhere near Danbury. There sat opposite me—I always like riding with my back to the engine—a young woman, masculine in most of the attributes of her attire; that is to say, she wore leather leggings and knee breeches. I looked no higher. Now, although I have been in this country quite often, I had never been in an American slow train before; and although I was quite aware that the *tempo* of New York is the slowest of any of the great cities of the world, I still harbored the superstition that once you were outside New York things might begin to rush.

Well, that train took hours. Hours and hours and hours. We have a very ancient story as regards our own Southeastern line that once a traveler asked a guard of a train why it had stopped. The guard said there was a cow on the line. An hour afterwards, the train stopping once more, the traveler asked the guard the same question. He received the same reply. On his remarking that there seemed to be a good many cows on the Southeastern, he was told that it was the same cow. Well, my progress to Danbury was like that. I grew so alarmed, so certain that we must have passed Danbury, that we must be approaching Portland, Maine, or even Halifax, Nova Scotia—I grew so alarmed that the one fear outweighed the other, and I asked the young woman—she was really quite plumply feminine and agreeable—whether we hadn't passed Danbury. She said with animation:

"Oh, why *didn't* you speak to me before? It would have been so much more amusing."

She gave me all the information about railways that it is usual to give a stranger who is traveling for the first time in your country. She told me, I mean, that here trains run upon steel rails, being drawn by locomotives whose propelling force is steam, that before entering a train you purchase a ticket, that iced water is supplied upon American trains, and that you can have paper cups for nothing—this showing a very high state of civilization. Then she told me that she was going to Kent County Reservation in Connecticut to catch rattlesnakes for the Bronx Park Zoo.

And what is more it was true. Now neither of those things would ever happen to you if you happened to be American and in your own country. But singular oddities have always presented themselves to me whenever I have traveled here. I don't mean to say that odd things ever happen so long as I bide put in New York, between, that is to say, the Battery and Eighty-fifth Street; nothing odd ever happens or presents itself to me, and I enjoy a relative immunity in Brooklyn or Hoboken; but let me once leave that, as it were home circle, to go into America . . . well, I will tell you how I went to Coney Island.

I wanted to take a Brooklyn rapid-transit line that had lately joined up with the Manhattan Beach Company. I paid the car fare, the statutory five cents. This was more than twenty years ago! At a given point in that journey a uniformed attendant remarked to me, "You hevn't paid your fare." I said, "I hev." He said, "You hevn't," so I paid him another five cents. Shortly afterwards a uniformed policeman came along and remarked, "You hevn't paid your fare." I said, "I hev." He said, "You hevn't," so he took me by the collar and threw me off the car. The train proceeded, and I observed that it charged into a crowd of mornamillion people. They, standing on the bridge over the river, were mostly precipitated into the stream.

By that time I was slightly discouraged as to my chances of getting to Coney Island by land. I went by water. On the boat I had nothing to smoke. I descended to the bar and asked a white-coated attendant for cigarettes. He said, "What sort of cigarettes?" I said, "What sort of cigarettes do you keep?" He said, "We don't keep 'em. We sell 'em." I said, "What sort of cigarettes have you got, anyhow?" He said, "We h'ain't got no cigarettes, but we carry a fine juicy line of Colorado stogies." I said, "Where do you carry them to?" and he said, "It's up to me now."

That would not have happened to you, neither would what followed. When I arrived at Coney Island I sought a dancing hall where, so I had been told, the entire population of the United States could dance in comfort, and with pleasure. (One does get told things like that when one is a traveler.) In the center of the otherwise completely empty ballroom a gentleman was slowly turning round, both his arms extended, and in each hand was a six-shooter, which he was discharging.

Now it is only to the traveler, by preference to the traveler who is not unlikely to write a book, that the gods vouchsafe such terrible joys. I should have said to myself at that date that nothing could have been more unlikely than that I should write a book about this city. My former visits here have always been either for sheer pleasure or on business, quite unconnected with my own writing; and were that not the case I should hesitate now, however hard I might have been pressed, to record my impressions of the city where people work by the forty-three or more, one on top of the other. For I have always found that if I went to a place on purpose to look at it I could either not write about it at all or only write about it quite badly. My job in life as I have conceived it has always been to record as passionlessly as possible my impressions of my own times and the places in which I have worked. And to say that I have worked in a city is practically the same thing as to say that I have at least liked it, for I have seldom been under the necessity of staying in a place that I did not like and in which I did not feel at home.

So I have always felt that my impressions were happiest when I merely glanced aside from something I was doing. Thus, Carcassonne has for me an extraordinary life because I wrote practically the whole of a book there—and indeed I have written a great many books in the south of France, and that is perhaps why I so much love the *Midi*, whereas places like Rouen or Tours or even Salem, Massachusetts, which I have visited avowedly merely to look at them, have left on my mind either very little impression at all or else impressions of a disagreeable kind. This is perhaps because the mere job of getting to places is disturbing, or perhaps because I dislike being the stranger anywhere. Thus Salem, to which I went on land and over water from Newport, R. I., comes back to me as a memory almost of detestation. It is possible that Gloucester, Massachusetts, which comes back to me as a memory relatively delightful, may be responsible for my dislike of Salem. That is to say that on the morning we went to Salem we were entertained by hospitable customs-house officers on board their launch—we were entertained with large quantities of raw salt fish which called for the consumption of almost larger quantities of their admirable champagne. Now if you consume large quantities of salt cod and champagne—I don't say there weren't also some crackers, but I don't remember them—if you consume large quantities of such comestibles on a steam launch between seven and ten in the morning, and if at half-past two of the same day after spending four and a half hours in the slowest, most dusty and dilapidated trains the world has ever seen—if after all this you arrive lunchless and with no prospect of lunch or even of a nice, hot cup of tea, at a beauty spot, the probability is that you will dislike that beauty spot almost more than you will dislike places which are called hells on earth. So it was with me and Salem. That journey comes back to me as a memory of intense depression and disgust. For the matter of that, it does not come back to me at all. I can only remember stopping off in atrociously hot weather at a place called Kingston-on-Thames, a railway junction, that was crammed with particularly nauseating French-Canadians. Kingston, as I remember it, consisted of one single shack, like an army hut, which proclaimed itself to be The Star and Garter Restaurant. The Thames was a trickle of yellow water between thirty-foot mud-banks. On our pushing open the gauze doors of The Star and Garter a long table revealed itself as covered with what appeared to be coal-black linoleum. But it wasn't. That linoleum rose and dissolved into millions of flies. So at half-past two we came to Salem.

Now all over such parts of the United States as I had already visited I had heard rapturous tales of the ancient beauties, of the marvelous old-fashioned hostelry, of the marvelous old-fashioned host of the inn at Salem. Alas, the most unpleasant place in England is called Ancoats, a soot-begrimed, coal-getting, cotton-spinning suburb of Manchester. Well, Salem intimately resembled Ancoats. It was black with soot and over it the skies wept sable tears. The entrance to the inn was a black staircase ascending between two shops selling things that I can't remember. But they were nasty things. The anteroom of the hotel resembled the most unpleasing of provincial railway-station waiting rooms, nor was there in it any single thing upon which to sit. Behind a counter snored an enormous man, his face covered by an unpleasant-looking handkerchief. We had to wake him to ask if we could have any lunch. He said, "Nope." We asked him if we could go to our rooms. He said, "Nope." We asked him if there was anywhere where we could sit down. He said, "Nope." He was the courtly old-fashioned host.

I may as well remark here that this is the most unpleasant thing I shall say about this country, where, generally, my lines have fallen in pleasant places. Moreover, I am writing about a time, nearly a quarter of a century ago, when American conditions, and particularly American rural conditions, were undoubtedly much rougher than is to-day the case. And I am also attempting to indicate rather how a book written by a foreigner visiting a foreign land should not be written than attempting to make any generalized point out of the oddities that I have recorded. It is obvious, I mean, that if one is about to visit a national shrine for purposes of observation one should not first fill oneself up with raw salt cod and champagne. Nothing could withstand those depressants. Not even Stratford-on-Avon. Or Chartres.

For myself, the first natural gasp of emotion at the sight of the buildings behind the

Battery or of the houses on the cliffs of Boulogne once over, I set myself to exhaust international similarities before beginning on the differences. That is perhaps partly a product of contrariety—of that spirit that the French call *ergoteur*—but it is at least self-consciously due to a profound feeling that those globe-trotters who are volubly outraged because it is difficult to find drinking water in Madrid or because hotels in the United States do not have your boots cleaned for you unless you ask for it—that such unthinking idiots do an immense amount of international harm. One must take into account that Madrid is situated in a country of great aridity and that labor in New York is relatively expensive before starting to cackle in the streets of either capital—and how much more before setting out to record one's impressions.

It is a curious fact that although we all look for instances confirmatory of the saying that there is no new thing under the sun, we are almost pained if we discover that our neighbor across the nearest frontier has not the habits and point of view of a Choctaw savage. We love it when we discover that the ancient Egyptians in their temples at Memphis had penny-in-the-slot machines that delivered perfume after the insertion of an obol, and enormous delight rewards us when we find in reading Bion or Moschus that the emotions of two women, one holding a baby, and both crushed in a crowd of sightseers watching a procession—that their emotions, gossip, and even their ejaculations are precisely the same as would be those of any two women with a baby watching a procession from the pavements of Broadway two thousand years later. But we are filled with disgust if the first Frenchman we see in a Paris restaurant does not eat his peas with a knife, or the first Englishman we see in Smithfield is not selling his wife with a halter around her neck. For why should we travel if we cannot discover our neighbors to be infinitely inferior to ourselves? Why, indeed?

For myself, having spent a great portion of my life in lands other than that of my birth and a great portion of my time in the study of historical documents, I am inclined to regard international or chronological differences as so slight as to be negligible or so changing as to cause an endless confusion. The inhabitants of the south of France in the thirteenth century spent the greater part of their days in baths or on other methods of perfuming and ablution. On the other hand, Brillat-Savarin, during the early decades of the last century, complained bitterly of the unpleasant smell of the inhabitants of New York, since in those days New Yorkers never bathed themselves and, indeed, the city did not then contain one fixed bath. So that how a traveler's book should be written I don't really know; I should never myself think of writing one. The results of migratory observation are so bewildering. The other day at a party an English newspaper correspondent was bewailing the fact that the passengers in New York public conveyances were grossly rough and brutal. He said that, traveling frequently with his wife on subways or in omnibuses, he had been disgusted by finding that if two vacant seats were separated by a third which was already occupied, the occupant of the third seat would never take the trouble to move so that my friend and his wife could sit together. He said that in England, on the other hand, this would always be done. He was interrupted by an American newspaper correspondent who stated that, having spent ten years in London and traveling frequently, he, too, with his wife by bus or tram, he had never once known the occupant of a seat that was between two vacant seats to make room so that a couple could sit together. At the same time I was experiencing an uneasy sensation. In the lounge of an hotel the day before, I had been occupying the middle one of three armchairs when two attractive young ladies came in together and sat one on each side of me. My natural impulse was to offer my place to the one or the other, and had they been elderly or unattractive I should certainly have done so. But I have lived for so long in France, where to offer your seat in a public conveyance to a lady below the age of sixty is apt to be regarded as an attempt to scrape acquaintance, that I refrained from that small act of politeness. What, then, are we to make of these divergent constatations? And, if those two young ladies were English, what did they think of American manners? There is no end to the way in which one is contradicted the moment one attempts any of these generalizations.

Last month I ventured into New England and, arrived at Boston, I delivered a harangue on the superior culture of the inhabitants of France. I said that if you talked to any French tram conductor you would find that he read books, took an interest in literature, and had very interesting views of life. That same afternoon I went by a slow train to a remote part of the state of Massachusetts. The conductor of the train was a benevolent individual, like a kindly, elderly English butler, except that I have never seen an English butler wearing silver-rimmed spectacles. He chatted in a fatherly manner with all the passengers, patted myself on the back, and appeared in every way like an English village patriarch upon an English village green. I almost saw a ghostly smock-frock draping his limbs.

Now one young man of that carload read sedulously in a magazine, and the conductor halted before him shortly after we had passed Fitchburg. The conductor asked the engrossed young man where he was getting off, and the engrossed young man answered that he was going to Fitchburg. The conductor said that he sure wasn't; that just as bees made honey for other folk to eat, so that young man's father had cooked his son's Sunday goose and others would consume it; that the reading of love stories in magazines was an engrossing pursuit but should not be indulged in when one had urgent business on hand. The assistant conductor declared that he had six times announced the name of Fitchburg. They discussed for a long time how that young man was going to return to his father's goose. He might make the eleven-fifty at the next station; if he didn't make that he would have to wait until the five-forty-two from somewhere else. Or he might take a trolley to somewhere and there find a motor-bus to within two miles of Fitchburg. That settled, the conductor began a monologue addressed mostly to myself. He said that books were engrossing things. When he took a book he himself would become so engrossed in it as to be completely lost to the world. Once when he was reading the *Decline and Fall of the Roman Empire* he had failed to go on duty altogether. He found love stories even more engrossing than history. Pictures also could engross him. He liked to go to picture galleries alone so as not to be disturbed in his contemplation. He liked the frescos of Puvis de Chavannes in Boston better than most other pictures he had seen. He then addressed the young man directly. The young man must learn from this from what trivial causes great events may arise. He pointed out that on that trolley car or on that bus the young man very possibly might pick up a young woman every whit as beautiful as the heroine of the love story in the magazine. The young man continually protested that he had been reading in that magazine not a love story but an article about Central Africa. The conductor, however, continued benevolently, that the young woman the young man would meet on the trolley would not only be more beautiful than the heroine of the story he had been reading but she would be an admirable helpmeet, a housekeeper of surpassing economy, and a cook beyond praise. Thus, by her savings as by her exhortations that young man would certainly grow to be as rich as my more famous namesake. He then again addressed myself. Life, he said, was like that. It flowed in a placid current for long periods. Then some trivial accident would occur, but accidents never arrive singly. And so on. He concluded by pointing out that that young man would pick up his young woman on the trolley and not on his car, because under his vigilant eyes the sexes feared to make each other's acquaintance, whereas the conductors of trolleys are less vigilant conservators of the public morals than their brothers of the railway service.

At any rate, after having uttered a panegyric on the Wattmen of France for their interest in books, pictures, and views of life, asserting by implication that no Anglo-Saxon vehicular public servant would be interested in such things, within the hour I had to listen to that monologue upon books, pictures, and life.

So generalizations are futile. They are, nevertheless, inevitable. I read to-day in my newspaper that a certain novel published in Paris concerns itself with "the lost generation of hard-drinking expatriates in Paris." Now it is my impression that compared with the Americans of New York, American expatriates in Paris are teetotalers. They have to be. Apparently—mind, I say apparently—in this country few people object to your getting far drunker than a lord at any social gathering. But in Paris if you get drunk at a party you are never asked to the house again. I do not think I have ever seen an American expatriate drunk in Paris. I do not mean to say that I have never seen drunken American tourists: I have seen thousands. But then I have seen thousands of drunken tourists of all nationalities in that unfortunate city—British, Swedes, all other Scandinavians, Martinique negroes, but seldom a drunken Frenchman. I do not think I have ever seen more than one Frenchman drunk. Certainly I have never seen a French woman overindulge.

So one generalizes. It can't be helped. But when one generalizes on international matters one should observe certain rules. One should, as far as possible, accumulate a large number of particular instances before attempting a generalization—and one should attempt to discover the reason that underlies that collection of similar particular instances. I am convinced that American expatriates in Paris, and still more in London, are a particularly sober race, because, as I have said, I cannot remember ever to have seen one of them in a state of intoxication. But my conviction gains immensely as soon as the consideration occurs to me that there is a reason for this sobriety and that that reason is a pretty strong one. And I think that another requisite for the writer of books of international comparison is what I will call the faculty of feeling-at-home-ness. In a beautiful passage in one of his books W. H. Hudson says that there was no place in the world, whether in New England, or in the Banda Orientale, in Patagonia, or on Sussex downs—there was no place in the world where grass grew and where there were birds in which he did not feel himself a son of the soil. And I may make almost the same claim for myself as regards any place in which men and women live. I might be inclined to exclude the nations with which we were lately at war. But even that I don't know. One of my reasons for disliking the Germans was this: at dinners given by professors in several German university towns where I lectured before the War I used to observe that, whereas the professors at table ate and drank enormously, their wives sat round the walls and knitted, and it appeared to me even at that date that a nation whose intellectual heads behaved in such a way must be in a low scale of the human race. But what was my perturbation the other day to read the following passage in a letter from an English lady who was revisiting Oxford and England after a long interval:

> I find, in spite of the cold, that I awfully like the aspects of the English country in winter, and of the towns, too. But *what* people! Dash and I went to the Magdalen Carol Singing on Christmas Eve and sat shivering in the ladies' gallery with the most unpresentable collection of completely self-satisfied women I have seen for a long time. The carols were not till midnight so we only stayed for "The Messiah," which I hate. But the old stones and the old woodwork are so lovely that one does not like them to be in the hands of pedants and frumps. Of course it *ought* to be a niceish society because there is neither great wealth nor great poverty and no one can *much* queer the other fellow's pitch. But it is no place for a woman. The whole concern has been run for the glory of

men since the beginning and women can only be domestic hangers-on. I felt that, sitting with the cold wives in the cold gallery of Magdalen Hall, watching their gorgeous husbands dining below with all that swanky simplicity of beer mugs, great fires, and bare tables that distinguishes the city of dreaming spires.

So I presume I must revise my estimate of the place of Germany amongst the nations.

Of course one can palliate the apparent brutality of the Oxford dons in Magdalen Hall by explaining that that is only a traditional game and that Oxford dons, being cultivated gentlemen, do not normally eat while their womenfolk fast; it is a platonic proceeding much as at Yuletide you may see elderly gentlemen of blameless behavior forcibly embrace young virgins under the mistletoe, and no doubt some similar palliation may be found for the behavior of the German professors that I used to find so disagreeable.

The chief requisite, in short, for the writer of books about other countries is that of comprehension—and not only the faculty of comprehension but the determination to apply it to every national or individual manifestation that the writer may witness. Looking through what I have written I find that some explanations are necessary. The old-fashioned host of Salem was no doubt rendered crabbed by being awakened suddenly from post-prandial slumber. I myself can be singularly brutal in similar circumstances, though I fancy you would find me normally bland and kindly. The reason why we could get no hospitality of any sort at that moment was simply that the waiters' trades union of Salem forbade any activity in hotels between the hours of two and six P.M. And the salt cod and champagne amply explain the desolate aspect of Salem which I believe to be one of the most delightful places imaginable. I quite believe it.

As for the singular instances on the road to Coney Island, it should be explained that those were due to that sturdy love of liberty which distinguishes the population here, native or resident. At that date the Brooklyn Rapid Transit Company had just amalgamated with the Manhattan Beach Company and, there being a law to the effect that only one car fare of five cents can be exacted for any single journey, the New York public was determined that it would not pay more than five cents for the journey from New York to Manhattan Beach. The companies had appealed to the law and had obtained from a judge, whose decision was finally reversed, a decree permitting them to exact two car fares for that journey. The judge, moreover, had lent the companies several posses of city police. So the public were up in arms against the injustices of this judge Jeffreys of the twentieth century, and if I chanced to poke my nose in between those contending forces, that was my fault. Foreigners should keep out of revolutions and civil strifes.

The young lady rattlesnake catcher is also explicable. Rattlesnakes will not breed in captivity, so an annual supply is needed for the Bronx Park Zoo if the inhabitants of New York are to be kept instructed as to the habits and aspect of those engaging reptiles. So every year a band of the young friends of the Bronx Park custodians proceeds to Kent County Reservation where the rattlesnake is protected and plentiful. Thus these young people secure for themselves a pleasant holiday whilst doing the state some service. The gentleman who fired off the revolver in the ball-room was not a National Trait. He had merely gone suddenly mad as has happened everywhere else.

The only phenomenon to me inexplicable was the lady on the *Paris*. I am still inclined to think that she was supernatural. In that case not the United States but an even higher authority must take the responsibility for her.

CHAPTER II

MY GOTHAM

IT used to be a saying in this city twenty years ago . . . "Little old New York is good enough for me." I daresay that is still a saying here. I have not lately heard it. . . . But in those days it was a good saying; it would not be so any longer now that the note of New York is that of a certain careless largeness—and a certain agelessness.

In 1906 New York had a quality of littleness and a quality of age. Then there were boarding houses where men in shirt sleeves and lady guests in white shirtwaists sat on the steps of houses in Madison Avenue right down to Twenty-fourth Street; then all along the main thoroughfares peanut barrows made harmony with their whistles—and, above all, every second or third passerby on Broadway was apt to stop and ask you—an obvious foreigner!—"Wal . . . and what are your impressions of New York?" . . . I assure you that they used to do that, and I assure you that they used to say "wal" instead of "well."

In these days no one asks you that; I suppose partly because New York is now a great city and partly because I, foreign though I be, am quite as much entitled to ask the question of the passerby as he is to ask it of me. I mean that whatever the city contains it contains no born New Yorkers. That is one of the phenomena that has here most struck me. I never meet born New Yorkers in the city of their birth. In Paris, yes!—in London, too, and in the remoter parts of New Jersey and Connecticut states . . . and none of the New York families that I used to know are here any longer. That I find sad, for they were such nice people. . . . Stay: I have met one born New Yorker who used to be here in 1906 . . . but that one—such a nice person too, was only on a visit here and has gone back home—to somewhere in Missouri.

These are merely personal impressions gathered in the course of conversation, and these are all that I have to offer. I am no statistician, nor would I be one if I could. . . . When I first came here I had a certain shyness about asking people where they came from, but later I observed that when two Americans meet for the first time they invariably ask, the one of the other: "Where are you from?" So I gradually contracted the habit. In England it is not done—I suppose because it is a matter of good form to pretend that every one you know belongs to a county family—and you have to pretend to know all about the county families of England. In Paris you can tell where people come from by their accents. As a rule it is Michigan; sometimes it is Nebraska, or else it is Sussex, England; less frequently Marseilles or Perpignan, France. There—in Paris—in the Quartier Montparnasse where I live, these accents are differentiable enough. I doubt if they would be here, where a sort of normal, not very noticeable accent seems to be developing.

New York is large, glamorous, easy-going, kindly and incurious—but above all it is a crucible—because it is large enough to be incurious. It is that that distinguishes the large from the not really large city. You become a Londoner in next to no time. You can even become a Parisian very quickly. I imagine you could grow into a New Yorker in a day or two. You could do that, indeed, in the old days. I remember twenty years or so ago being taken over a public school in New York by an inspector. In one corner of an asphalted stretch of playground stood a small boy sobbing. Says the inspector to him: "Why are you crying, my little man?" Says the little boy: "Me brother hit me." The inspector: "But you mustn't cry because your brother hit you!" And the little boy—with ferocity: "I ain't going to let a blame Dago hit me. I'm a New Yorker, I am!" His brother had been born in Warsaw, he himself on Ellis Island. Perhaps to-day it doesn't go so easily as that!

But above all, for me—and I am talking about *my* New York—the note of this city is its casualness, its easiness, its sheer ordinariness. In the old days one would not have been much astonished if Redskins had raided Central Park; to-day one is astonished if anything out of the ordinary happens.

The most singular proof of this came to me the other day. Some one had made an engagement with me—a "date"—to meet him at a certain business house at a certain hour, on East Twenty-seventh Street. The business house, as is not unusual, had moved to other premises. There was nothing for it but to parade the street in front of that vacated nest—for half an hour or more. For myself, I always arrive a quarter of an hour before my date; no New Yorker known to me was ever less than an hour late for an appointment. Well, I began to do sentry duty in front of that store—stepping up and down and about—turning, as the drill book has it, in a smart and soldierly manner. But gradually I began to think and gradually I began to loaf. I was thinking out, as a matter of fact, what I am writing now . . . so that at the last, it was from miles and miles above the clouds that my arriving friend had to haul me down. . . . A comfortable, warm feeling that was. I might have been in Kensington Gardens, London, England, or Rue Notre Dame des Champs, Paris, France . . . just anywhere, in any great city.

And— No: my pocket was not picked. And— No: no trolley car mounted the sidewalk to crush me, and no one jostled me, nor did I once have to step aside. I just mooned happily.

The New Yorker thinks that he rushes. He doesn't, and with the slowing down of the traffic added to the always leisurely pace on the sidewalks, he can't. Neither does the New York business man hustle. In London or Paris when I go to see my lawyer or my banker or my publisher I dash into his inner room, feeling frightened at my temerity. I tell my business in a few seconds and I rush out—sure that I have taken up too much time: reading it in the stern, bored faces of my interlocutors. Here, bless you, in palatially appointed rooms, the business man appears rather as orator and anecdotalist. Before each announcement of what he is going to do for you he makes a preamble as to his moral and social motives—a long preamble! As you try to tear yourself away—appalled at the amount of his time you have taken up—he grasps your extended right hand gently but firmly and holding on to it, he tells you six anecdotes about his family, two about his last game of golf and several more about how they hustle in this city. Then he suggests taking you out to lunch somewhere —with a short round—twelve holes or so— afterward . . . It is the paradise of business men. They say money is here easy to make. It must be!

And it is good enough for me. . . . As I have already said, in one of his books W. H. Hudson asserts that wherever grass grows and there are birds he has felt himself at home. For myself, I have something of the same feeling wherever men and women are to be found. In France I feel myself a Frenchman, in Italy I feel more than half Italian; I am almost entirely Provençal in Provence. I daresay if I ever go to America I shall feel myself American enough. But I have never been to America: only I feel at home in New York.

Americans, in fact, terrify me a little. But

I am fond of New York and fond of several of the inhabitants of this city. I don't know that I am fond of any one else in the world—outside of my family, of course. The French don't offer themselves much for fondness: the English don't much understand what to do with it. But New York and New Yorkers like being liked . . . they let you know it and that is agreeable.

New York, then, is a place where I can moon about and feel pleasant—much as I can in Provence. What it is—this city—I don't presume to dictate, but I do presume to say that it differs very little from any other great city, psychologically.

I see my English friends walk about here, agape for differences. They are astounded that bus conductors push something like an automatic pistol at them instead of handing them a pink strip of paper; they find it queer that the subway is not as deep down as the Tube in London, and unnatural that houses should scrape the skies. But the nature of man is not changed by having to stick a coin into a little slot or even by working in an office on top of forty-three other offices. . . . New York differs from London in having a keener intellectual life; it differs from Paris in that intellectual circles are smaller. Perhaps the products of the intellect are less valued here by the bulk of the people than is the case in other cities—but New York is becoming more and more of an intellectual center as the days go on—and that adds enormously to the world. It adds enormously, not merely to the pleasure, but to the safety of the world. If I—or you—can sit—as I found myself thinking the other day—perfectly tranquilly at table with eleven other people, all foreigners to me, and if I can feel perfectly at home and can find myself talking quite unself-consciously about just such things as I usually talk about at home, it is a sign that a great step has been taken toward that union of peoples that the world so dreadfully needs.

One day—may it come soon—there will not be any America, there will not be any Europe; there will be just the World about which we shall all move at ease, where we shall all loaf and think and, please God, find money easy to make. Well, one hears eternally that New York is not America. It is obviously not Europe—the Atlantic lies between. Is it, then, the outer fringe of America—or the end of Europe? Perhaps, the one overlapping the other, here we have the beginning of the world.

I like, at any rate, to think of it like that and it is possible that it is true enough. For

New York is Babel without confusion of tongues. A place of refuge for all races of the world from the flood of ancient sorrows; the forlorn hope of humanity that, having lived too long, seeks rebirth. And indeed, the note of New York—its gayety, its tolerance, its carelessness is just that of a storming-party hurrying towards an unknown goal. It is the city of the Good Time—and the Good Time is there so sacred that you may be excused anything you do in searching for it. That is an ideal so practicable!

Happiness, the quest for islands of the Blest, the pursuit of saintliness, of sanity or of tranquil continuity—all these graspings after a Fata Morgana have from the beginnings of eternity, in the Old World, given weariness to the lives of mankind. They are so difficult and no New Yorker contemplates difficult things. But the Good Time —like the Catholic religion—is human and attainable. How it may be with America I do not know; perhaps there the sterner virtues and pursuits for which stand the pilgrim fathers—who were not Americans— still obtain. But not in New York. It is the only place outside Provence where everybody is rich and gay. But yes . . . outside, the sterner virtues still obtain. I was just now airing my amiable views of New York to a lady from Boston. She said: "Yes, but to be rich and gay is not the supreme end of life." . . . For me, alas, it is! I do not mean for myself personally . . . but for nations and races. Races that are not harassed are seldom menaces to their neighbors; races that have leisure have leisure also for Thought and the Arts. And it is pleasant—it is the pleasantest thing in the world, to think of great numbers of people —great, great numbers of people—all enjoying themselves innocently. You know that when you think kindly of Henri IV, who wished that every peasant of his realms might have a fowl in the pot on Sundays. It is assuredly not from New York that any menace will come to the world: it is from places where the sterner virtues obtain.

By day the soaring cliffs that rise joyously over behind the Battery are symbols not merely of hope but of attainment; after dark, and more particularly in the dusk, they are sheer fairyland. There is something particularly romantic in a Germanic sort of way about mountains illuminated from within. I remember watching the mountains behind Caerphilly in South Wales from Cardiff; their purple black against the night was pierced by illuminated and flickering minemouths and the suggestion that gnomes and

Nibelungen of sorts were there at work on the veined treasure of the earth was irresistible. But it was a relatively heavyish glamor: the millionwise illumination of New York is a lighter, gayer affair—as it were Oberon and Titania against the Germanic gnomes. The mind on seeing it connotes not subterranean picks and sweat, but lighter, more tenuous occupations—the pursuits of delicate, wayward beings. And indeed, the mind connotes correctly enough, for though statistically New York may for all I know be a great manufacturing city, nothing could be further from *my* Gotham, except for the work of the stevedores in the Port, than those other desperate and mournful labors, in the dark and underneath the earth. For New York stands for air and light. Preëminently for air and light.

But, for me, the most vivid recollection of New York—and I have it even when I sit here at work in one of the darkest, oldest and most Bloomsbury-like houses of the downtown of this city—is the view, long ago, from the roof of one of the tall houses that look down on City Hall, of the brand-new, marvelously white and beautiful Flatiron. In those days the Flatiron was one of the seven wonders of the world and the air was more clear than it is possible for air to be, beneath the crystalline bowl of the sky. The shadows were all naturally blue, too, and every detail of every cornice of that building was visible from where we stood, pinkish white outlined by delicate blue. And indeed, every detail of every other building within sight was equally visible, distance being indicated only by the diminution of objects, not by their growing dimmer to the sight. And each building had its *panache* —its ostrich-plume of steam streaming away in the keen wind. I have never known greater exhilaration; I have never seen anything more gayly beautiful.

All that is very much changed now. There is, I suppose, a good deal of soft coal still being used, and what has been used during past times of stress seems indelibly to have left a film over the white buildings and even to have taken the edge off the very clearness of the air. The buildings round the Woolworth Tower, seen even from the distance towards Sandy Hook, have no longer their pristine whiteness; they have rather the gray of bones that have been long exposed to the air, though they still tower proudly aloft, man's protest and assertion in the face of Nature.

New York, I think, has lost a little in impressiveness, if not in beauty. Painters—

and particularly foreign painters—still rave about her canyons and ravines. But there are too many. They give the painters greater choice of "bits," but to ordinary humanity they are apt to produce at last an effect of drafty gloom—as if one were at the bottom of shafts rather than on the face of the friendly earth. And the contrasts of the old days are lost.

It used to be a cumulative affair; you used to come down on the Fifth Avenue horse-stage between personable but not too lofty houses; then you plunged into splendid abysses. And the sentinel before these splendid abysses was the Flatiron that, seen down either Fifth Avenue or Broadway from afar, was as white and as radiantly proportioned as any Greek conception for celebrating a victory. That used to be a journey; a romance.

To-day the Flatiron is gray and the skyline along Fifth Avenue where it goes along Central Park is too uniform in height with the rest of the city to let you have any feeling either of entrance or of plunging down . . . Heaven knows where, on the North, you would have a sense of entering New York. She straggles out into sparse suburbs and wilted rusticities as is the case with London towards Twickenham, or Paris, Montmorency way. So that the compact, comfortable feeling that one used to have, of being bounded on the two sides by the rivers and of entering a city that was still low at Fifty-seventh Street, is gone for ever. New York will never be little and old again; she has assumed the ageless aspect of the great metropolis.

It was, no doubt, merely an illusion, but the feeling that one then had that, when looking downtown from Central Park, one was outside the city walls and was looking into it, was so strong as to be nearly irresistible. There were obviously hundreds of thousands of people dwelling behind one's back; one knew even individuals who lived just next door to the great baseball ground —at 118th Street, I think. But the New York that mattered to one was before one's face. The fluxes and refluxes of residential New York are so continuous as to be absolutely unfollowable; but I am inclined to think that the people that one knew when the Flatiron was still a prodigy and Madison Square the fashionable shopping center, and Sixth Avenue below Twenty-third Street housed great stores, and poor Fourteenth Street itself between Sixth and Third Avenues was old-fashioned and "residential"—the people that one then knew lived between the southern boundaries of Central Park and the south side of Washington Square. I remember having letters of introduction to or calling on one or two families on that Square, several in Gramercy Park, one in West Fourteenth Street itself, others in Twenty-sixth and Thirty-sixth Streets, and so on upwards to the Park. On the other hand, the offices of my publisher were in Twenty-third Street between Broadway and Lexington, and he himself lived somewhere up in the hundreds, and I had several friends away in Bronx Park. I stayed, I remember, at first in the Waldorf-Astoria, then in a hotel on West Twenty-seventh Street, just off Fifth, which was more than indifferent. Its anteroom always smelt of fish frying in indifferent fat.

I remember this particularly because of a gentleman who, somebody told me, was a Western Senator—but I daresay he was not. He boarded a trolley on which I was progressing from Wall Street to Twenty-seventh—at about Eighth Street. The coat-tails of his frock-coat flew out behind him as he made a flying leap onto the vehicle; he wore an immense black sombrero, a scarlet tie and black leggings. At least, I like to think of him as wearing leggings; perhaps he did not really, but I confuse his memory with that of Buffalo Bill. He seated himself beside me, drew from his tail-pockets an immense dark-scarlet apple, which he first polished on his sleeve and then held under my nose.

"Ain't that a peach?" he exclaimed. I regarded it with attention and then remarked that it appeared to me to be an apple. He remarked that if it was not the peachiest peach he ever seen he never seen another. And he added:

"Take it, mister." I refused to take it; I said that if I put it in my pocket it would spoil the set of my coat, whereas if I carried it in my hand it would make me conspicuous. But that fellow pursued me all the way to West Twenty-seventh Street, got off the car and followed me into the ante-room of my hotel, holding out the brilliant apple and vociferating: "If *she* ain't a peach I never seen. . . ." And over the deep humiliation that I felt at being seen in such flamboyantly attired company was superadded the nauseous consciousness of that ancient fish-and-burnt-fat smell. It has never left me.

And next day one of the papers came out with a column headed in gigantic type: "English Peer Cannot Understand How Apple Can Be Peach." It was accompanied by a caricature of myself entitled: *The Animated Match.* In those days I weighed only nine stone two—123 pounds. Alas, alas!

I used to think for long that that caption gave the measure of the little oldness of my Gotham of those days when English visitors for pleasure were so rare that every one of them had to be dignified at least with the title of peer. Indeed, when I told the emigration officer on the steamer that I was visiting the United States for my pleasure and in no hope of gain, he simply refused to believe me. He said he had never heard of anybody doing that. . . . I remember him vividly to this day. A fat, dead-white complexioned man, with silver-rimmed spectacles, an unbuttoned waistcoat over an indecently enormous abdomen and wearing a singularly shabby straw hat, he lolled sideways at a table before which we stood, smoked a cigar and cleaned his fingernails whilst he spat out questions from behind his cigar. As the first United States official to give an impression to the first visitor coming for pleasure he was a bit of a misfortune. But, as they used to say—for I have not heard the expression in many years: This is a free country.

And yet I do not know—as regards that heading. It seemed to me the note of a small old town that the papers should give columns to an incident so trifling. Yet I was the other day in Chicago, which is neither little nor old, and which can never be either. Certainly it can never be both—for when it was merely Fort Dearborn it was little and after the fire it was young. But nowadays it grows vaster and vaster—and younger and younger and younger till it begins to have that pathos of extreme youth that. . . . However, I am not writing about Chicago now; I am writing about its hawk. For when I was in Chicago lately the whole city, all the newspapers, all the streets were convulsed or rendered impassable by a hawk.

This bird of prey had been driven in by the severe weather in the surrounding Middle West, and making a home on the crags of the Tribune or the Wrigley buildings, it was striking down at leisure the city's innumerable pigeons and eating them here or there in full view of the populace. And that was "Front Page News" *in excelsis*. No war tidings could so have caused the larger sort of type to spring into use across the tops of pages of journals. The streets were rendered impassable by reason of the crowds gazing into the skies and dangerous because lovers of pigeons fired charges of gun-shot into the air at imaginary hawks, whilst lovers of hawks thrust their arms up or down whilst they were in the act of firing. That lasted for days.

I don't, by the bye, write of this with reprehension or scorn or anything. It seems to me very proper and right. Life in the great towns is so mechanical, so aloof from vitality, so much a matter of machines that any incursion of the natural—of the wild, the predatory and the free—is a very proper derivative. It will cool blood heated by overindulgence in refrigerated food and brains overtaxed by tickers and typewritten statements. European nations support their royal families and aristocracies for this purpose; why should not Chicago have its hawk and its gunmen—though indeed the hawk excited more attention than ever did the raid on the Drake Hotel?

Still, excitement over accipitrine or foreign visitors for pleasure may be taken as the characteristic of a small old town, as a rule. You cannot imagine New York or Paris or London raising an eyelid because of the visit of a hawk to the City Hall or the Mansion House or the Hotel de Ville—though I do remember that years ago London was stirred by the first visit of great flocks of seagulls to the Thames Embankment. But that excitement was soon over;

to-day the gulls are so familiar a part of the riverine landscape of London that hardly a soul is found feeding them. Occasionally some one will take them a bundle of scraps, and now and then a city clerk at lunch time will toss into the beak of a gull a scrap of the sandwich he is eating as he strolls. But then, whatever be the case with Paris, New York seems to have no city-consciousness at all. London, indeed, has herself precious little. The Parisian is always the Parisian, but the Londoner, except that he will exhibit symtoms of mild disgust if you suggest that he could be anything else but a Londoner, is singularly unaware of the existence of his city. And the New Yorker—so battered at, apostrophized and continually rebuked is he by all the rest of the inhabitants of God's Country—the New Yorker outside New York only very coyly admits the place of his residence. He prefers to say that he is from Vermont. Or Nebraska.

And—for it is pleasant to contemplate the inter-actions and reactions of great cities one upon another—what of city-consciousness London has has always seemed to me to come to her, at any rate in part, by way of New York. By way of the gray squirrel! For it was when the gray squirrel was first set free in quantities in Regents Park that, in order to secure immunity for them from the acts of chase of the London small boy that the London County Council issued orders that the board school teachers were to inculcate lessons as to civic pride upon their pupils. The teachers were to tell their pupils that gray squirrels were things to be proud of because other fellows' cities had no gray squirrels. And so with other beasts and birds. So that to-day the fauna of the London parks is profuse and astonishing and you never see—as used to be the case in my boyhood—the London male young using catapults against living things except other small boys—and perhaps cats. So here again the New World redressed the balance of the Old.

And more than redressed it. For one thing has always caused a note of sadness to me in New York—the fact that I seldom see a bird here. And for me a city without birds is like a house without a piano—something a little deadened. I seldom—practically never—see even the humble, troublesome sparrow in New York. Even years ago that fact used to impress me. One went along the streets and never saw a bird. There were, however, other beautiful flying things. One day I went into the office—in Twenty-third Street—of my publisher, and he said—it was Mr. S. S. McClure of prodigious memory:

"What in h—ll have you got on your derby?" So I removed my billycock, and there, right in the front, in the place usually occupied by a regimental or a fireman's badge, was a great, beautiful moth. A great moth with a wing-spread larger than that of a sparrow. And, after that I used to take pleasure in observing those fine things floating with the boldest and most beautiful flight in the world—smoother than that of the finches and more floating than the swallows—over the buses on Fifth Avenue or round and round the trees of Madison Square in an autumn season. I have not seen them lately—but that, I am aware, is no proof that they are no longer there. For sitting the other day with a lady in the window of the National Arts Club looking down over Gramercy Park—which in London would be called a square—I remarked to her that New York had for me always a certain note of sadness because there are no birds here—not even sparrows. She remarked drily:

"If you will give yourself the trouble to look down you will see at least seventeen." And there they were—at least seventeen sparrows flying across the gray winter grass of the square. There was even a pyramidal box pierced in tiers with small holes and supported on a pole—a miniature sparrow-cote.

But although, for that moment I was caught out, I do not believe that that little company of seventeen sparrows in Gramercy Park need convince me that New York ever is or ever could be a thickly bird-populated city. Yet somehow the companionship of birds is a necessity to my complete pleasure. I do not mean that I have—or that to be a proper man any one need have—the passion for birds that was our dear Huddie's—W. H. Hudson's. I should never have the patience to watch for hours and days and weeks a titlark's nest in which a cuckoo had laid an egg. But in the garden of my studio in Paris there was a colony of white blackbirds, and in a thorn tree in the backyard of my flat in London a thrush nested. And it was a pleasure to me to glance up from my work and see the wings flitting intimately past the windows or to see on the leads the mother thrush with her yellow, black-speckled waistcoat, dropping smashed snails into the enormously distended beaks of her clamorous nestlings. It gave a touch of lightness to the day.

But if here I look up amid the shadows

and out into the backyard I see nothing—a cement floor, an incredibly begrimed glass roof of an open shed. And it is just a well; except for soot, clean but eternally Cimmerian. A well—for, although the house I have chosen to live in is old and relatively low, on the other three sides that surround my yard there tower up the skyscrapers, and I live either in funereal shadows or in artificial light.

Do not mistake me. I am lamenting neither my lot nor my lodgings. I have had the offer of a perfectly brand-new apartment on Park Avenue. But I should die in a perfectly brand-new apartment on Park Avenue. Here I have a number of largish, tall rooms, dark but with sculptured marble mantelpieces and roughish Early American furniture—honest early nineteenth century journeyman's work such as might have been produced in Kent or Sussex in the England of that period. It is a fact that I have been in this rambling, ramshackle old place four months and only yesterday discovered that I was the proprietor of a kitchen. I wanted to give a tea-party and asked the housekeeper to lend me a spirit lamp to boil the water, whereupon she said:

"Why don't you use your kitchen?" And there it was.

This will seem incredible and I have not time to explain it; it is nevertheless a true anecdote. For what I am talking about is the tall buildings—the skyscrapers of New York. By way of birds. Where a sparrow *can* lodge a sparrow will lodge—but on the faces of these immense cliffs there is not lodgment even for a sparrow—except maybe, skywards. You see, I have been gradually raising my eyes towards the tops of these cliffs by way of the backyards and the shadows. I will confess that it was the hawk at Chicago that first made me fully recognize the vastness of these affairs. For when upon the railway platform of Rockford, Ill., I read in the local journal that Chicago, toward which I was proceeding, was convulsed by the visits of a hawk, my first and natural reaction was to think:

"Why don't they kill it? Or at least take it alive?"

I read that every shotgun and rifle in the city had been mobilized; that the Chief of Police had issued ukases alike against the shooters and the hawk; that the commissioner for something had declared at all costs that the hawk must be protected because the overpopulation of the city by pigeons had long been a menace to the health of the human inhabitants; that the deputy commissioner for something else and somebody else had spent the day spreading clapnets on the roof of the City Hall and baiting them with live pigeons; that the local agriculturists had passed resolutions declaring that the hawk must be protected because pigeons eat the grain from sown fields; that the mobilization of the city fire brigade had been advocated in order to spread bird-lime on lofty roofs, but whether to catch the hawk or the pigeons I do not know ... when on that windy platform I read all this there rose in my mind's eye at once the image of a London suburb, far-flung, with its two or, at most, three-storied villas. No London commuter would notice the hawk; if he did he could not tell a hawk from a hernshaw—or from a pigeon for the matter of that. Or if they did see it on a roof and want to kill it, it could be done with a boy's catapult. Almost with a pea-shooter.

But till then I had never seen Chicago. I had heard that her suburbs, too, covered an immensity of ground, but I had reckoned without the Wrigley or the Tribune or the other tall buildings that have above the mournful plains of the Middle West the aspect of being a great assembling of super-lighthouses, the one whispering in the ear of the other. Or of an immense basalt, fluted and pyramidal crag aspiring to the peak of heaven! When I did see them I realized that to kill a lone hawk that had those altitudes at its disposal would be about as easy as to kill one hawk on Seawfell ... a one and only hawk. And then I had a better image of New York herself. For the lower levels of New York are familiar enough to one and so indeed are the higher office-chambers. One walks the streets or visits the offices gaining those associations that in the end are what make a city seem alive to us. But I wonder how many of us ever raise our eyes to the heavens or think of the skyline in inner New York. Few, I imagine. At any rate, it was not until I lately saw Chicago that I had a vision of the immense plateau that the New York roofs must make. For till from a distance one sees the Illinois metropolis one has little idea of what the isolated skyscraper is like—and until one has fully taken in an isolated skyscraper one has little idea of an assemblage of them so serried that their roofs form a plateau. And the idea of that level of the air is singularly stimulating.

One has, naturally, long ago heard the legends. It is several years since I met a man who told me that his father made a living—and a good living, too!—as custodian of the roofs of unfinished or as yet not fully occupied buildings, living thereon in a temporary shack. Later one began to hear of millionaire owners of vast edifices who had bungalows on their roofs, poplar groves, garages, I daresay, golf courses . . . who knows what? That sort of imagination is very easy to have and to cap. There is no reason why you should not have a lake with sailing boats. Indeed, the swimming pool of the Illinois Women's Athletic Club is on the roof of a Chicago skyscraper.

That sort of conception and the putting of it into execution are easy enough if you have enough money and a sufficiently large slave population. Even Babylon had its roof-gardens—far away and long ago. And it is a mere commonplace that where space is very valuable the rooftops will be utilized be they four stories high or a hundred and fifty. So will the earth beneath ground and the very rivers. For I am certain that, in the end, the East River will be covered in, since, sooner or later, New York must either succumb or find more breathing space.

New York is what she is because she is in part an unofficially administrative, in part a pure pleasure city. The days are no doubt past when all the business men of the United States had to go on their knees to Wall Street to obtain capital which Wall Street would grant or not according to its own sole will and caprice. To a certain extent the local Federal Reserve banks from Alabama to the State of Washington suffice for necessary loans, and Wall Street alone can scarcely create or quell financial panics for its own pleasure. Nevertheless, immensely the larger part of the financial and commercial transactions of the Continent are transacted either in or through New York and she is still the financial center of the New World, as London is of the Old. Indeed, a curious parallel might be drawn between the situations of the two great banking cities. New York is not, of course, officially the metropolis of the United States: she houses neither the Federal Legislature nor the Federal Judiciary—but that she is the "capital" of the United States in the colloquial sense in which that word is generally used no one not a much more than a hundred per cent American would deny. And probably by her combined social and financial pull she controls the Legislature at Washington far more than is acknowledged.

That, however, is not my topic of the moment—nor is it ever likely to be. What I was about saying is that it seems fairly obvious that New York cannot continue—whatever her position of control may at present be—*in* that position of control unless she does attain in one way or the other to more elbow room. I said lately that the New Yorker never keeps an engagement to within half an hour—but that is not to accuse the New Yorker of having an unpunctual mind or of lacking the desire to be of a royal politeness. It is merely to point out that, hurry as he may, and with the best will in the world, he simply cannot do it. There is *no* gauging the time of your arrival at any given point on the ground level of the city. Having an engagement for half-past four in Sixty-fifth Street, I took a taxicab one afternoon at four in Madison Square and arrived at five minutes past five, having traveled at the rate of practically a minute and a half to a block. The same evening I had a date for eight o'clock in the same street. I took a taxi at the corner of Sixteenth Street and Sixth Avenue at seven o'clock and arrived at Sixty-fifth Street at seven-twenty—having to cool my feet for forty minutes outside the house where I was dining and having covered the ground at the rate of practically fifty blocks in twenty minutes.

Those were merely social engagements, so

MY GOTHAM

that it was only my own time that was lost. Supposing, however, that they had been business dates! I should not only have lost my own time but I should have kept the man who was expecting me waiting in addition for thirty-five minutes.

And this goes on millionwise: there must at present be thousands of millions of business hours lost in the city of New York every year, on the surface of the ground alone. It is all very well to say that you can always take the Subway and the Elevated—and I believe that this course recommends itself to the democratic spirit of the American. At any rate, when I said to a lively young lady from Seattle that I never moved about New York except by taxi or by surface bus, she retorted on me as if I had been more than several sorts of a snob. But to do it, if one's work makes any call on the individual, is not to be any sort of a snob at all. If your work is individualistic in nature —and I presume that the work of big business heads and the like *is* that—you must have privacy of a sort for as long periods of the day as are attainable. You are an engrossed person. I can do twice as much work as most of my confrères in New York —or in London and in Paris, for that matter —just because I do protect my thinking machine by such devices as taking taxis whenever I have to move about the streets of such cities as New York. . . . This, however, seems to call for a new chapter.

CHAPTER III

SKYSCRAPERS

IF you take the population of a small town, say thirty thousand souls who are usually spread over houses bordering on several miles of road—I believe that if you wanted to walk over all the roads of London Town it would take you two hundred years at four miles per hour!—if you take that population and crowd it all into one house having a frontage of say sixty feet of say sixty-foot road, you will find that that road-space is singularly little for the needs of that population when another population of the same size is housed just a foot away along that same road. You will increase the bewilderment if you consider that of the population of a rural township of thirty thousand, about two-thirds—the children and the housekeeping women—use the roads very little, whereas your thirty thousand will all be active movers using their sixty feet of sidewalk and the sidewalks of their neighbors at least four times daily and all at about the same hour of the day—in tides.

The congestion between—to be liberal—eight and ten of mornings and four and seven in the evening will be terrible. In addition there is the lunch hour. That is the situation of New York.

Now, do not be mistaken: I *like* the skyscrapers; in their splendid congeries they are beautiful, impressive and above all—for me—thrilling as can be. I wish the word "skyscraper" had not been invented for them; its suggestion is one of ugliness that makes the superior European hug himself for his superior virtues. He does not do anything ugly to the skies, he says. But these great, beautiful pinnacles aspire to the skies and the clouds caress them. It would indeed be better if the European would regard them as cloud-houses, though the term is too clumsy for everyday New York to use, the initial of the word in common use taking the sound along faster.

But do not believe that I am, from a superior standpoint, criticizing my Gotham, any more than a timid lover is criticizing his divinity when he deferentially suggests to her that if she continues to lace so tight and run up the stairs so fast something painful may happen to her. The simile is in fact a rather exact one—for New York *is* laced too tight and would if she could get up the stairs at a terrific rate. But she can't. She has not got any stairs and her elevators are terrible time-traps. I will admit that I am absent-minded and not infrequently push the "up" button when I wish to be transported to the solid ground. I daresay, indeed, I do it as often as not. But the other day I was on the fourteenth story of an office building in the shadow of the Woolworth Tower. Now fourteen stories is no extravagant altitude as altitudes go, nevertheless it took me eleven minutes before I was on the sidewalk. That is to say I waited ten and a half minutes in front of a great range of blank doors above which red lights flashed and went out. At last one of those doors above which no light had flashed drew back and, by running hard, I managed to make it and insert myself before it had disappeared. Nor are you to imagine that that was a small or dud office building; it was great and housed a whole United States State department; nor was I specially incompetent. There stood in the monumental corridor beside me, alike waiting for means of descent, one of the remorseless-jawed, clean-shaven, gray-tweed suited representatives of the Big Business of this country. When we had waited seven and a half minutes he said "Damn!" several times between his teeth; at the ninth minute he said that if he had back all the hours he had wasted in waiting for these contraptions he would have time to write a book.

The sentiment came home to me. For only two days before I had remarked to the doorkeeper of a speak-easy, at a quarter past two whilst awaiting an English authoress who had promised to lunch with me there at one—I had remarked in my haste that if I had back all the time of my life that I had spent in waiting for women and the money I had thrown away in overtipping I should have no need either for the fountain of youth or the wealth of Henry Ford.

Be that as it may the time wasted in New York over waiting for people who are late for their dates, over waiting for elevators, during traffic jams and over answering purely frivolous telephone-calls must amount to a very considerable expenditure if it could be represented in money. Let us put it in another way: If I go to London, or if I go, in Paris, from the South to the North Bank, in both cases on business, I expect to —and I do—get in at least three, but not unusually four, business interviews before lunch and at least two, but quite frequently

SKYSCRAPERS

three, afterwards. In New York if you can manage two before lunch and one afterwards you are lucky, simply because of the difficulty of transit and of synchronization. I am not of course speaking from my own sole experience.

In addition, at the present time, the postal service is very unreliable and the telephone more exasperating than that of any other great city with the exception of Paris. But the astonishing thing is how, in these matters at least, New York changes. Twenty years ago under Colonel, I think, Waring and his White Wings Brigade New York streets and sidewalks were the cleanest in the world—cleaner than those of Middleburg itself. Three years ago, during the Keep Smiling Movement the telephone service was like Heaven. One telephoned for the pleasure of it—the pleasure of hearing the nice voices of the operators and of coming in contact with anything so smooth-moving and efficient. You spoke to Boston or San Francisco on the Long Disstance and it was as if your interlocutor was sitting in the room with you. To-day to telephone to say, St. Louis, is a torture. I was doing so this morning. Apparently I was just audible in that city but that city was completely inaudible to me. When I asked for a better connection the operator spoke very rudely to me and took several minutes to give it to me. It was better, but in the middle of a sentence we were cut off for over five minutes and the operator was still more rude. And, the conversation finished, the company attempted to charge me for the three minutes during which we were waiting for the better connection and for the five during which they had cut us off—and all at a dollar fifty a minute! And twelve dollars are three pounds. And it is to be remembered that conversation carried on in circumstances of exasperation are seldom very serviceable.

The New York internal service is little better—and gone are the cheerful voices of the operators and the agreeable local accents! To-day when you ring up you hear coming back to you a sort of weary Cockney drawl that repeats your number twice all wrong. Then you are put onto a third wrong number. That is just like London, just as your Long Distance experiences here will be just like those with Trunks in England.

Now these are not grumbles. I personally care very little whether the telephone service be efficient or no and I could very cheerfully dispense with it altogether. Indeed I am being driven out of New York by the ceaseless ringing that goes on on my telephone all the morning when I ought to be working. That is a fact. I am leaving New York much sooner than I wished to do because of the too efficient telephone—and I do not like the thing that drives me out of New York, and indeed out of America.

Not grumbles—but speculations as to a certain queerness! Why is it that twenty years ago you could eat your dinner off the Sixth Avenue or any other pavements—and if you left any crumbs behind within the minute one of the Colonel's men in white would miraculously appear and sweep them up; whereas to-day. . . . Well, last Sunday but one I walked after lunch from 36th Street along Sixth Avenue to 16th and I have never imagined that such filth could be found in a city street as there we had to walk on. The paper repositories in all the side streets were piled high with *immondices* of an intimate and unmentionable kind and these with every conceivable other disgusting object overflowed from the side-streets onto the Avenue itself. And the queer thing was that although I was hardly able to desist from retching and wished incontinently to take a taxi, my companion—of a normally more delicate nature—said, no, the exercise would do us good and accepted the garbage as being all in the day's journey. That sort of patience in the face of abuses is symptomatic—but of a characteristic that must be written about later.

Again I say that this is not a grumble. I prefer New York with soiled pavements to other cities set upon floors like those of Heaven. It appears that the streets are in this condition only on Sundays because the street-scavengers on that day employ a holiday—or at any rate it is only on Sunday afternoons when the streets are nearly empty that their condition jumps to the eye. And for myself it is not difficult to arrange to stop in bed on the Sabbath. It will do me good. . . . But *why* these changes?

One is accustomed to say: "Oh well, you cannot expect to have a perfect telephone service on this side of Heaven," but New York *had* a perfect telephone service. Only three years ago. . . . I suppose really on a given date some years since one of the iron-faced ones who here direct great enterprises, strolled into the chief exchange and remarked: "Hello, girls, keep smiling!" and then took certain steps to see that they jolly well did. But, since then, he must have gotten another craze, or have forgotten, or have been promoted—or immersed in crossword puzzles. . . . It will have been something like that; thus changes occur and affect the lives of millions.

Changes. . . . Well, to me it is immaterial whether New York remains the financial centre of the Western Hemisphere except that one likes, irrationally, the cities that one likes to have predominance in even immaterial things. And it would make me mournful for at least ten minutes if, in that respect, St. Louis or Dayton, Ohio, or Seattle or any other place should usurp the supremacy of New York. At the end of that time I should have assured myself by the employment of reason that I cared nothing about the matter.

In these matters human psychology is very queer. I suppose that everybody who knows anything about them laments the decay of the ancient glories of . . . well, say Spain. It is sad to think that never again will the great galleons trail away into the golden sunsets. London to me to-day is nothing—or next to nothing. I know nobody of its seventeen or so millions—five people perhaps outside my own family. New York really means a great deal more: my memories of her are nearly all pleasant . . . full of clean air and white Flatirons. All the same if some one—in Chicago, usually—tells me that New York—or more usually Chicago—is larger than London I feel a tinge of regret. For the only quality left to London is its largeness—its far-flungness . . . and its regrets. Immense, mournful and black-robed, she is a sort of Queen Victoria—a colossal Widow at Windsor amongst the cities.

So she should remain. But still more if the world is to be habitable for . . . oh, for men of goodwill, must New York retain her financial supremacy amongst the American cities. To me financial supremacy means nothing except if it means that in financially supreme cities life is rich and gay and Thought and the Arts can subsist on the crumbs. Apart from that, Wall Street might, for all I care, emigrate to Norfolk, Va. And yet it mightn't. It is pleasant to think that, amongst all her other bewildering delights, New York has that distinction. . . . I regard all bankers with distrust as being the root of most of the evil of the world; all financiers outside bankers I would export, as was done with the dogs of Constantinople, to a small desert island where they might subsist on each other's flesh. But it is difficult to see how New York could do that and keep at the bottom of the trunk that medal of the empty renown of Financial Supremacy. . . .

Precisely like one's war medals. One keeps them in bits of brown paper, tossed into a valise amongst old footwear, tubes of tooth paste and mildewed, forgotten papers. Occasionally, when on one's travels, one searches for a supplementary shoe-horn and digs to the bottom of the valise, getting a glimpse of the bright ribbons and the metal discs. For a second, then, one has satisfaction. . . . Atque ego. . . . Oneself, too, once. . . .

So New York must retain her Financial Supremacy if there is to be no crumpled rose-leaf in the mattress. . . . But how can she if the skyscrapers are to continue to crowd one upon the other? In order to boss the Big Business of the Western World you must be able to do *some* business. For myself I entertain a profound disbelief as to the business activities of the Big Business man. Outside his office he hustles like anything, but inside it he sits smoking immense cigars and reading eighteen newspapers. His feet will be either on or not on his roll-top desk. When they are not on it they will be hanging over the arm of his chair. Meanwhile in another room his stenographer will be reading and answering his business correspondence. From time to time he will dictate a golfing or other social date into a dictaphone; he will use his telephone for the purpose of telling his barber to reserve for him the chair in which he will spend the hours from eleven to one. That is why he has his alabaster complexion.

He will use the Subway or the Elevated partly to show that he is a democrat, partly to show that he must save time. But then he has the time. Nevertheless, if his immense Firm is to continue, his stenographer must be able to have at least one business interview of a morning and one every other afternoon with luck. That is about the present rate. But when all the new skyscrapers are put up and when the Hoboken tunnel permits all the new road traffic to pour into the city from that side. . . . What then?

Except sentimentally it is no affair of mine. Solutions of problems are found somehow. No doubt double-decker streets will come and prove some palliative. Or the filling in of the East River nearly as far as Brooklyn Suspension Bridge might solve the problem. The trouble is that the very thing that makes New York so attractive—its want of corporate self-consciousness—militates against the problems ever being consciously tackled. The late New York elections turned, not on congestion, on defective posts or exasperating telephones; not even on begarbaged streets. They turned on milk, dragged as an unavailing red-herring across the track because the Opposition apparently had not the courage to raise the religious issue.

That of course is only a fugitive—a temporary—instance; but the indifference to corporate matters is apparently a permanent condition. Only once in the last four or five months have I heard anybody in New York speculate as to the future of New York as a corporation and that was when some one at a very Conservative Club offered to make a bet that within twenty years there would be a Jewish mayor of New York. He found no takers. His hearers hated the prophecy but no one proposed to do anything about it.

And that is very characteristic of New York—and indeed of the Eastern Seaboard generally. You will hear all Boston groaning about the Irish domination of Monsignor O'Connell and his myrmidons; that city under a slight snowfall is such a hell of slush and filth, even on the Hill and round the Common, that civilization for the time to all intents and purposes is at an end. For all the women of Boston must wear the clumsy horrors called slickers thus assuming the aspect—not of Europa, who was carried off by a bull—but of a human feminine population that should have been forced by a malign wizard to have the feet of cows. . . . But perhaps that is not evidence of a breakdown of civilization; perhaps it means only that His Eminence who watches over the city of the Tea-party is determined to preserve the chastity of his cure. He doubtless figures that it must be difficult to love even one's dearest and fairest when she has assumed cow's heels. . . . Ah, but it isn't.

Yet the Cabots go on speaking to God and nothing is done about it. For myself, all Papist as I am, I could not live in Boston and bear those circumstances without doing something. Why, even the other day, on Beacon Street with my shoes full of water and having walked round five or more blocks in the hope of getting onto the Common and so to Newbury Street . . . even I for a moment had the insane impulse to free the city by some rash act. Being of the race of Hampden and the Pilgrim Fathers I thought of hitting a policeman. For in England if you wish to redress a grievance you hit a policeman and then tell the magistrate all about it, the court reporters seeing that your grievance is aired in the public press. . . .

But the Boston policemen are all Irish, carry formidable clubs . . . and dislike the English.

I remember being, years ago, on the Common with a compatriot. As we approached the statue of Washington he—my gifted friend—said to me:

"Look at our distinguished fellow-countryman!" And an Irish policeman who overheard him remarked to us:

"If you say dat again I'll hit ye wid me club!" and twirled his weapon by its string round his fingers.

It was perhaps his memory that saved his present-day descendant. At any rate I did not hit one. . . . Be that as it may I should not like to say how many times I have not been moved "to do something about it" in this country. Indeed, not ten minutes after, in a restaurant with still soaking feet, I was vowing to myself that I would shoot a certain kleagle not many miles away from Boston Common. The Ku Klux Klan was at that moment—could one believe that it was actually in process of happening at that moment?—insolently and abominably oppressing a Roman Catholic lady of my acquaintance.

It was an incredible situation. There the Hub of the Universe—the poor old Hub of the Universe!—still with its red-brick London houses and its red-brick paved sidewalks, its Hill, its Common ... there it still was with all its odious superiority and its still more odious snobbishness, but prone beneath a rapscallion Papist domination that must be as unpleasing as the world has ever seen. And yet, not twelve miles away the exact Ghibellines of those Guelfs were proposing to tar and feather an innocent family of my co-religionists! Because they employed a negro handmaiden in their store!

That of course is politics with which I do not mean at the moment to meddle, though I do not mean to funk it when the time comes. The image that immediately I want to get onto paper is that of proud cities of immense populations surrounded by States of immense populations that are practically at war with the citizens of the proud cities. Here you have New York surrounded by that whole population of *all* the States of the Union—and all the populations of all those States detest her with a detestation compared with which the detestation of the ordinary Parisian for the city of Berlin is as very little. Or, *in petto*, you have the once proud city of the Lowells more completely de-Lowellized than would have seemed possible fifteen years ago, but surrounded by a patient agricultural population dominated by a secret organization representing what I will call Lowellism at its very worst . . . representing the very worst type of Puritanism, the very worst of Anglo-Saxondom, of terrorism, of bullying, of ignorance and of intolerance.

That is all right; the United States likes to have things so and it is no one else's affair. It is a phenomenon like another. But what is queer is that the nice people—the nice, quiet, decent people who are of neither of these Houses support with such patience quite intolerable interferences . . . and intolerable inconveniences. It is as if one should be in a lovely, lovely house subjected to a plague of flies, and, asking why there are these flies, should be answered that it is because of the dunghill under the window . . . and, asking why there should be the dunghill under the window, should get no answer at all.

But there it is with all its queernesses. For, as I have said, if you ask a Chicagoan why *his* snow is not cleared away with the lightning rapidity of a New York snow clearing he will reply that it is because the New York municipality is corrupt and employs an unnecessarily large army of overpaid snow-cleaners in order to get their votes; if you ask a New Yorker who knows anything about Chicago—but there are very few of these—why it is that his streets are cloacal wildernesses of filth on a Sunday whilst the streets of Chicago are brightly clean on all days of the week he will reply that it is because the Chicago municipality is corrupt and vastly overpays a huge horde of Sunday street cleaners in order to get *their* votes. . . . There does not seem to be a great deal of system about it. I know cities in another hemisphere that are corrupt enough in all conscience but *their* municipalities when budgeting for the year budget for cleanliness, pure water, efficient tramways and reasonable sanitation *in addition* to corruption galore. And that would seem to be the only satisfactory way—that relic of the feudal system. For, if the citizens of those latter places are not kept relatively comfortable they begin by hitting policemen and if that does not bring redress they hang a municipal councilor. But that is seldom necessary.

But there you are. The lovely ladies of America in patience parade the winter streets in slickers; my poor nice R. C. friends think that because they know a Number One or some Klan official they may be allowed to keep on their store with its negress handmaiden. If they may not they will have to sell their store which has been in the family since the days of the Pilgrim Fathers—for white assistance is not procurable. But they regard the prospect if with regret at any rate with patience. Certainly they do not propose to do anything about it.[1]

I think I have already said that I like New York. If I have not yet conveyed that to the reader's intelligence I will here repeat that I would rather be in New York than in any other place in the world except Provence, to which I retire in order to recover from the effects of too much delight. And after all the proof of the pudding does lie in the eating. It takes, no doubt, *all* those ingredients of the United States to make the dear nice friends I have in that place the dear nice people that they are. I am afraid of America—and I and the world will go on being afraid of America. But the thought has crossed my mind that *they* are nice just because America is so formidable. If you ask the New Yorker why he puts up with a set of circumstances that he regards as an oppression he will reply that it is because two aged and enormously wealthy persons wish that set of circumstances to prevail and that whilst those two aged billionaires wish

[1] The store has been sold.

those circumstances to prevail prevail they will. (I am not advancing those statements of the New Yorker as facts but merely as the not unusual statements of the New Yorker.) He will go on to say, mournfully, resignedly and with a far-away look in his eyes, that all these stresses, these oppressions, the terrifying aspect of America as a new and worse Prussia jack-booting it across the world—all these things come from hundred-per-centism, which was invented by gentlemen with names like Hunderttausendstrassenheimer, from the Klan, from those impressed by the fact that one gentleman possesses a Complete Billion and above all from the terrible small-town ladies with silver-gray hair, Roman noses, protuberant shell-rimmed glasses—from the terrible ladies who are the most oppressive and the most reactionary feature of hundred-per-cent life.

So speaks the New Yorker. . . . And when he so speaks my mind always provides for myself the corollary: "But in the end, my dear, they have given us You!" For whatever New York is or is not, she, like her other greater—for she is still by a million or so the greater—Great Aunt, Greater London, is incontestably an ark of refuge. A sanctuary. You go to New York as in the middle ages the victims of the Law, the King or the Vehmgericht fled to the altar. Alsatia ... I figure ourselves—us, New Yorkers and their guests—who stroll in Central Park or hurry joyous, arm in arm, along Fifth Avenue between say the Cathedral at Fiftieth Street and the Waldorf Astoria. ... And surely Fifth Avenue between Fiftieth and Thirty-fourth Streets is the loveliest Street for its life and light and gayety in the world. ... I figure ourselves as irresistibly recalling to the mind the gay, insouciant, idle strollers who, far away and long ago, in one Alsatia or Durham or another had escaped from the Wrath to Come and, cleaning their nails with their sword points, leant against sunbathed walls and jested at Time, Fate, Virtue, Law and the Seven Woes of the World.

And in the end that is the true consummation of Anglo-Saxondom. We, the true Anglo-Saxons—the real Hundred-per-Centers whose names are other than Hunderttausendstrassenheimer or Putz—we are not only Saxon and Norman and Dane, we are Jew and Huguenot and Hussite and Anabaptist and Pilgrim Father and Absconding Bankrupt and Younger Son and Jansenist and Circumnavigator. We are, we Anglo-Saxons, from London to New York and

Sydney and Hongkong and Delhi and back again to the Strand by way of the Boulevard Montparnasse, we are all the Bad Hats of the World. We are the Eternal Nuisances of Everywhere who have been kicked out by Everybody and we have traveled the world round and round and round and round again in search of the City of the Good Time. . . . So the sunlight falls on Fifth Avenue between Fiftieth and Thirty-fourth . . . for Us and there is now our Spiritual Home.

That is not merely lyric: it is historically true. Spitalfields silk; Bradford wool; Boston beans . . . all the famous commerces of Anglo-Saxondom are the products of Heretics and Nuisances to their kings and Countries. Flemish Protestants, French Huguenots; English Dissenters made those places and those wealths. The First Anglo-Saxons; the first Danes; the first Normans and the first Isaacs of York and London Lombard Streeters—they were all the restless expatriates of the Universe. To-day you have New York—which is not America. . . . Well, in the old days you had Provence—which was not France.

The Westward current has by now pretty well finished. The West itself and still more the Middle West according to the New

York theory is ruled over by tyrants compared with whom Charles I or George III were village policemen and by tyrannies compared with which that of the Russian Bureaucracy or the Council of Ten of Venice were village Sunday-schools. That is no doubt an exaggeration. But it is true that the sense of it is there. The American visitor goes to New York in much the same mind as that of the Englishman visiting Paris; he returns to his Main Street no doubt very little modified. But the American who settles in New York becomes at once an ex-American. That would not be the case were his Main Street more supportable to him. And from then on his wistful kin remaining behind regard him as the lost soul . . . the Expatriate. To what exent his abandoned home exercises a pull on him it is obviously scarcely for me to say. That, naturally, differs with the individual.

But he remains the New Yorker, because He is New York. He is why New York is no longer either little or old. He has determined that she shall be large, loose, easy and tolerant, because he is the reaction from the small town, the cabined frame of mind and the pressure of personal supervisions. And that liberty he enjoins on all the city. It is all very well to say that New York is the largest Jewish city in the world, the second largest Italian, the third largest German and the only large Irish city—or whatever statistics may allege. It is also true that if you sit in Bronx Park on a Sunday or walk down Sixth Avenue below Twenty-Third Street on almost any evening you will not hear a word of English. . . . But you will not meet any but New Yorkers and it will be very New York Yiddish or Italian or German that you will hear.

They say that whole tracts of America, more particularly in the Middle West, are almost purely Scandinavian or that great tracts of New England, I think, are irremediably Polish—the Poles resisting more than any other nationality all Americanizing influences . . . and why should they not when it has been for centuries only because of their powers of resistance to alien influences that they have existed at all? Nevertheless the Italian quarters of New York are tremendously New York and very little Italian; the Jewish quarters are much less Jewish than is Whitechapel; the Syrian quarters are New York with just a few odd-looking inscriptions in the windows.

For the moment I do not feel strong enough to expose exactly what I mean—or rather that particular exposition does not at the moment fit in with my plan. What I want to point out amounts to this—that a man who has settled in New York, and only for the shortest of spaces of time, is irrevocably altered . . . and altered always in one direction as is the case with groves of trees planted on elevations where the prevailing winds are mostly the same.

It is all very well for some one who has never been much in Italy to say that the Italian quarters of New York resemble Naples; they do not. They resemble New York where some Italians live . . . and grow less and less Italian. And nothing is more impressive than to observe how, gradually, the home notes, the home remembrances, grow less and less vivid, less and less tenacious. You talk to the Italian who brings up your firewood twice or so a week and under your eyes he grows less and less a son of Fiesole. He has to make efforts to remember; his ambition is to transport Italy to New York—practically never to return to the banks of the Arno. His father had eleven children besides himself. He has by now brought seven of them to New York; this summer when the wood-faggot trade is least active he will return to Italy . . . and bring two more of his little brothers over to

New York. ... Or go to any—to the most —French restaurant of this city. ... There used to be Wishing Wells of which it was said that he who had tasted of their waters not only never rested till he tasted of them again but was never thereafter the same man that before he was. And indeed the action of New York upon humanity is perhaps more observable outside the United States than within them. You see the New Yorker in Lombardy, on the banks of the Rhine, on the shores of the Mediterranean, and, though he have been born in Milan, Coblenz or Toulon, he is marked out from all his fellows and his own people: he is the Americano, or the Amerikaner, l'américain. The other day in a *café* of a Mediterranean maritime port a rather questionable individual approached me and addressed to me a rather unsavory proposal in an irreproachable local *lingua franca*. Nevertheless something—a scarcely discernible nasality, I daresay, made me say: "Vous avez habité New York?" He answered: "Oui, Monsieur, j'y ai passé quelque temps." I said: "Moi aussi," and there came into his eyes the slightly dreamy expression of one who reflects upon the time when he first tasted of the tree of knowledge of good and evil. It was a strong bond between us, but since

his avocation was one which does not commend itself to the good citizen I did not further pursue the acquaintance. . . .
For myself. . . . But that perhaps would interest no one but myself!

CHAPTER IV

IT IS NOT SO MUCH THE PLACE . . .

THE other day I lunched at the Brevoort *en tête-à-tête* with a very distinguished writer. Being in New York we were very much rushed for time so we talked for three hours about Style. We discussed the methods of writing of every writer under the sun . . . except two. Then we strolled along Fifth Avenue northward, still discussing Style. Writers do sometimes do that. At the southeast corner of the intersection of the Avenue and Fourteenth Street, just as he was stepping off the curb to take his trolley-car he halted with one foot in the air and said: "I have read your books: I like them very much." So I said: "Well, I have read your books and I like them very much, too."

So that angle of that street has its pleasant association for me. Crossing onto the corner immediately opposite on a very slippery day I once had a very bad fall—so that corner, too, has its clothing of memory. The northwestern corner and the pavement going from Fourteenth Street to Sixteenth witnessed one of the happiest moods of my life; I remember going along it with almost dancing feet, which does not so often happen to me. At the tobacconist's store that used to be at the remaining corner I used to do my telephoning when my own telephone was out of order or when I did not wish to be overheard by the other inhabitants of my apartment. So that corner vibrates in my memory with the recollection of such exasperations, despairs and resolutions as only form themselves in the broken conversations of those appalling instruments. I must have said more insulting things to business agents and have uttered more agitated rudenesses to private persons in one of the little boxes of that store than I can have brought forth in any other place in the world. That store is now gone; pulled down; made over.... So with its Chesterfields and Camels and chewing gum and telephone boxes it is, with those conversations and their remembrances, covered with the patina of the Past. The results of some of those conversations are still active in my life, nevertheless.

At a coffee-shop at the corner of Sixteenth and Fifth Avenue I used for long to breakfast on coffee and baked apples, opening and reading my letters meanwhile—letters for me often as momentous as the conversations at the other corner—though indeed the habit of correspondence is so nearly dead between the East River and the Hudson that most of the momentousnesses of persons not in physical confrontation are apt to be telephonic. Still I had my emotions seated on the high stool at the counter—there, too. . . .

And I remember, years and years and years ago, a particular walk from a quiet, old-fashioned maiden lady's house in East Fourteenth Street. . . . Along Fourteenth to the corner where I lately had that conversation, crossing up the east side of Fifth Avenue and so up, across Madison Square— It was then almost just after the murder of Stanford White and one had there to talk of him and the Madison Square Gardens that are now lamentably gone—and so up into the Twenties—the then glamorous Twenties.

Well, the results of that particular walk still dominate my life as writer and as man —perhaps almost more as writer than as man. For it was a couple or so of days afterwards when walking along the opposite side of the Avenue between Twenty-Second and Twenty-Third that looking across at the Flatiron and remembering something that had been said on that particular walk there came into my head a sudden, half-philosophical, half-literary idea that has ever since formed the chief basis of my technical stock in trade and the mainspring of my actions.

It would be superfluously biographical at this point to dilate on that idea. It is sufficient to say that very early on an October morning of strong damp shadows, looking across at the almost forbidding, dumb, purplish column of the Flatiron whose side towards me was in the deepest shade and feeling at the moment a mood of intense loneliness, I suddenly conjured up on that then deserted opposite sidewalk the figure of the companion who the day before or so had been walking with me at the foot of that same Flatiron that now seemed a barrier of gloom between myself and a desirable sunlight. And it occurred to me to think how the imagination of that figure made the Flatiron suddenly alive for me whether as an architectural mass or as a figurative barrier between myself and the sun. . . . And I realized that, if the day before, I had not found the Hudson above West Point as beautiful as the Rhine—and for sure the upper defiles of the Hudson *are* every whit as beautiful as the Rhine!—it was just simply because, for me at least, there was no human figure whether of my past or my imagination that I could set up against the reaches of that stream as I could for the Rhine where it enters the mountains above Coblenz. . . . And I began, standing there, to apply the same process to moral and philosophical ideas. . . .

In effect that is why when I wish to give the effect of a city or the exact incidence of a moral apophthegm I try to do it with an anecdote, essaying the rendering of the turn of a phrase or the twist of a crooked mouth rather than with any generalization of a loftier or a more academic kind.

You may say that that is because I can not bend the mightier bow of the professional philosopher or statistician and that may well be the case; nor indeed have I the least ambition to inflict this rule of my own life and my own art on any other persons that live or write. But it seems to me true that a city will be dear to you if it have human associations and that if it have none it will be nothing but a pile of stones however phantasmagoric in arrangement.

That is why the occupation of the tourist seems to me to be a very empty affair. . . . But I am aware that the rule is not universal; for the other day, happening to express to a mildish elderly lady, that very view—that the Hudson was less stirring than the Rhine because of its relative lack of human interest, I was positively overwhelmed by the vigor of her reply. She said that whenever time, weather and money served her, she fled off to desolate regions far, far beyond the Grand Canyon or New Mexico and there, habiting herself in men's breeches—it gave me as we say a turn to imagine any one so mildly feminine in breeches!—she bestrode the first mustang she came across and rode out for weeks into the desert. To avoid traces of humanity.

So there are other views. And I daresay that in America the ideal of confronting bitter, untrodden deserts is stronger than elsewhere. But that can hardly be true of New York or its inhabitants. The ideal of the he-man smiting a hairy breast as he confronts a wilderness of solitude is there prevalent enough and you may as like as not be pushed off a trolley by the elbow of such a male pursuing his ideal. But it *is* an ideal rather than a practicable rule of life otherwise he would be throwing you over the edge of a canyon rather than merely back into Third Avenue.

Be that as it may it is obviously rather

the attraction of the population than that of the landscape that brings people to New York. . . . When I was first in this city I adopted or invented as a protection against the persons who on the sidewalks persisted in asking me what were my impressions of Gotham the phrase with half of which I have headed this chapter. A stout man, in a light brown alpaca coat, an immense abdomen, sheltering itself beneath a green-lined sunshade, wiping his streaming brows in the brilliant sunlight of West Twenty-seventh Street, would anchor himself like a rotund buoy in front of me and begin: "Wal . . . " But before he could finish his question I would say: "You know . . . it isn't so much the place as the people." And with my diaphanous nine stone two I would pass on, leaving him with his wet handkerchief suspended in midair, turning in slow bewilderment in the sun on the sidewalk.

I do not know what has become of that type of man who used to be *the* typical New Yorker of the shopkeeping class any more than I know what, precisely, I meant by that particular smartness. The waters flow under the bridge and the little stones find their places, so he is gone along with Stanford White and Jem Sullivan and the Pa of

Peck's Bad Boy and the domestic tranquillities of Fourteenth Street. But I know now what that sentence means.

For it *is* not so much the place as the people. The place is not really so much to write home about: the sights of New York are relatively negligible. I mean as compared with those of let us say Rome. When you have said the skyscrapers you have said most of it. Michigan Avenue offers a finer prospect—or in three years' time it will—than Fifth Avenue; the Terraces of St. Louis a more dignified domesticity than Riverside Drive; the Hill at Boston, if you are Anglo-Saxonly inclined, is more like Hampstead than New York's Chelsea, where I sit in glooms writing, is like Chelsea on the banks of the Thames or than Greenwich Village is like the home of the Bloomsbury School. . . . And if I would rather sit here and write than sit and write in any of the other places it is rather because of the people I shall meet on the sidewalks and still more because of the associations that will assail me at the street-crossings than because of anything in the architectural line that I shall see—or even because of the effects of light and shade in the deepest canyons. I could forego all them.

But the queer power that New York has

of clothing itself in those associations and of assembling those people—that is her real, strange, triumphant note. She changes so fast that you cannot at any moment say: "This is my New York." And yet your New York it remains. The tobacco-store at the corner of Fourteenth Street vanished in next to no time after I had begun to use it as a means of communication with the outside world—but it collected an extraordinary crop of associations and became part of the Past with a rapidity such as could have been equaled in surely no other city. And you may say the same of all New York. Impressions are all there so vivid that what, in another place, would leave next to no impress on the mind becomes between the Battery and Central Park of almost epoch-making importance. So New York clothes herself.

I have pointed out in another place that, being no architect, I do like stones to be covered with moss or ivy and that, in consequence, Paris round the Arc de Triomphe de l'Etoile really repels me. The stones of New York are no less machine-sawn, hard and antiseptically resistant to the growth of lichen. But, no doubt because one thinks—or at least feels—quite twice as fast in front of the buildings of Fifth Avenue as before the stones of the Avenue de Wagram, Tiffany's, say, will clothe itself with a shimmer of more remembered emotions than will all that Paris avenue and the Avenue Hoche added to it.

I am talking of course of personal not historical emotions, Naturally if you are of the type that can only find emotion in the contemplation of spots where Marie Antoinette or Madame Roland or Ney or Landru were executed New York will relatively little excite you. You can feel like that at Lexington; the stone on the Common is more than impressive; the shot there fired *was* heard round the world. But Lexington Avenue is about all that New York offers you in remembrance of that explosion and it is curious to consider how when, reminiscently, you look back on the faded social glories of Fifth Avenue it is practically only the names and figures of actors that come back to you. Or of course Dempsey fought Sullivan on East Fourteenth Street if I am not mistaken. Or was it Sharkey?

And I have been on—or at any rate somewhere near—the spot where Hamilton fought Burr and I have even been in the beautiful house in Charlton Street from which Hamilton issued forth to that contest in New Jersey. But that house will no longer exist when these pages are in your hands and I do not know that it cut much ice whilst it still stood. And neither the days of Andrew Jackson nor of Lincoln nor, for the matter of that, of Cleveland or Harrison seem to have left much social impress on New York. When I was young and for some time after, the Vanderbilts and the Astors were the great names of Fifth Avenue; below them stood the actors, the Players' Club being the most thrilling social place to which the young visitor could be taken. You sat there at the next table to the immensely great and the unspeakably chic. You can still sit there in the old house in Gramercy Park—but you might be at the Garrick Club in London where your dim thrills come from the faded type of ancient playbills and improbable oil paintings of the Infant Roscius as Tamburlaine.

It is certain that my conviction gains immensely as soon as another soul can be found to share it; and, looking through the reminiscences of a gentleman who must have rubbed shoulders with myself on the Fifth Avenue of my slimness, I see exactly the names and exactly the restaurants mentioned that would have sprung to my lips if I could ever remember any names at all. . . .

IT IS NOT SO MUCH THE PLACE ... 111

There, in those columns they are, the Astors and the Vanderbilts ... and then the Thespians, John Drew, Ethel Barrymore, Maxine Elliott, Richard Mansfield, the Otis Skinners ... all of them promenading along Fifth Avenue as far down as Twenty-fifth Street, lunching at Sherry's, tea-ing at Martin's. (For they *did* tea even in those days in New York, though you could not at Newport, R. I., as I remember to my discomfiture!) Dining at Delmonico's; rehearsing anywhere along middle Broadway. ... I remember an extra-rehearsal of Richard Mansfield's; during a heat-wave and at two in the morning he called his company together and in tones of hollow-mouthed impressiveness said: "Gentlemen and ladies, I insist that in my theatre no one shall perspire. Let there be no sweat!" *Tempi passati! Tempi passati!*

I had meant indeed to allow myself to write more of those days when New York was little and old and Sam McClure's Magazine as great a power as *Maga* a century before in England—with its Miss Tarbell and Miss Cather and its youth and glory and beauty and resounding muck-rake. ... But Mr. Irwin has hopped in before me and done it naturally better.

But had I done it it would not have been

as presumptuous as it sounds in a foreigner and visitor. For me New York as City has changed relatively little. I know that this is contrary to the general idea. But I find my way more easily about the part of New York that I frequent than about the part of London that I used to frequent, and the parts of Paris that I used to know at about the same time seem to me far more changed than either. In New York at least the streets are permanent, change the sky-line never so much or so rapidly—but consider what used to be where the Boulevard Raspail was only a very few years ago. . . . No, it is not so much the place as the people that has changed: or, if the city has changed the people have changed infinitely more.

I happen for sentimental reasons to have visited—or to have gone merely to look at, at first an old residential house and then the buildings that have occupied the site of that house. Well, the street occupies the same position; I can go to it now blindfold from here. There was once there a brownstone basement house, with steps ascending, and a stoop. Its chief occupant came straight from Cranford, England; its Nottingham lace curtains, its brown furniture, its Wilton carpets were testimony to an immensely old New York gentility that need in no way bow

IT IS NOT SO MUCH THE PLACE ... 113

its head before Beacon Hill. It had mahogany doors, round-domed china cupboards, generous staircases; at Thanksgiving time its relatives came all the way from Concord, Mass., and from Philadelphia to pay seasonal and obligatory visits. It gave way to a saloon of sorts and the street in which it stood became so bibulously dangerous on account of the prizefighters and their hangers-on that for some time I had a certain timorousness in going to look at the site from across the way. It lasted like that during several of my visits. Now it is an innocent, very crowded cheapjacks resort where Jewish young men offer incredibly colored foulards, socks, braces, corsets and minor garments on completely unarranged, piled up trays. Still it is not difficult to find as would be the case with the house of a professor of mine that I used to call at somewhere between the rue de Fleurus and the Luxembourg. Even the locality there is forgotten.

But its occupants were, in the first place, born New Yorkers with the habits, the attractivenesses, the grave social manners of a caste that had existed for generations and generations. They were already a little impoverished and added to their incomes by discreetly affording shelter to strangers—

nice strangers who came from Tennessee, Pittsburgh, Portland, Maine, and the South. . . . Well; they are all gone—to Paris, to Versailles, to the more remote parts of the State of New Jersey, to the cities of the Middle West. Only one of them still inhabits for a part of the year one of the old Bloomsbury-ish named streets to the west of Sixth Avenue, far downtown.

One may naturally exaggerate—one does. I wrote lately in my haste that since being in New York for this present visit I had only met one born New Yorker. That was true at the moment; but I met my contradiction only an hour or so after that statement of mine had appeared in one of the Sunday supplements. For whilst I was having tea at a party at the house of a lady with a Knickerbocker Dutch name in a large very modern apartment I was addressed by a reproachful gentleman who bade me cast my eyes over the other guests at that party. There were perhaps thirty. Every one of them including himself, he asserted, was a born New Yorker and not only that but owned and inhabited the property on which he or she had been born. And going out to dine in the same neighborhood later on the same day I was assured by the charming wife of my hospitable host that her husband not only owned and had been born on the property of which the flat in which we found ourselves formed a part but that that property had belonged to his family for six generations.

I am bound, however, to add the corollary that every one of those people—or at any rate of those to whom I was privileged to speak—stated that they were going to move out of New York. They were going to live either in London or in the further country districts of the New England States. New York had become too much for them.

And they are no pioneers, for of all the New Yorkers that I used formerly here to know and who used to own their own properties and have much the same social habits, not one remains or perhaps one daughter of one family remains. I do not mean to say that all these New Yorkers have abandoned or intend to abandon all contact with New York. They remain within practicable motoring distance in the surrounding country—within, as it were, the sphere of influence of the first-nights, the concerts, the picture-shows, the dog- and horse-shows ... and the medical attendance. They remain to that degree New Yorkers and where your social contacts are there is really your domicile. For, indeed, even London and

Paris may be said to be within motoring distance of New York and I am frequently astonished to find to what a degree ladies resident within reach of Bond Street or the Rue de la Paix prefer to do their shopping from Thirty-Fourth Street upwards, during swallow-flight visits. I don't say that they are right: I don't, indeed, say that they are wrong in preferring the beautifully dressed, more *pimpants* shop-fronts of Fifth Avenue to the austerities of the more august Houses across the water. Even for a man to shop in New York is twice as exciting as to shop in Paris. I know that I have been induced to spend more on haberdashers in this city in a few weeks than in any few of the last years in the Ville Lumière—or in London either for the matter of that.

But the point is that the expatriated New Yorker remains at least as much a New Yorker as the Londoner who leaves London remains a Londoner, or the Parisian a Parisian away from the boulevards; their minds at any rate go back to those pavements when they think of adornments, possibly when they think of youthful glamour and romance . . . and certainly when they think of the future. For I have been astonished to find in Europe how, be the New Yorker never so apparently hardened a European—be he or

IT IS NOT SO MUCH THE PLACE ... 117

she never so indurated by the ways of Courts, Good Families, the English Country House or the Almanach de Gotha—he or she will unshakably stick to the idea that their children at the impressionable age must go back to New York and get their maturings presided over at least by New England institutions. That is unshakable.

And it is obviously not criticizable by me. If I had an English-speaking son or daughter to educate decoratively it would seem to me to be indifferent whether they went to Oxford or Harvard or Poughkeepsie or Newnham. If on the other hand I had a son or daughter whose future seemed to necessitate that instruction in technical matters that in certain circles is to-day called education and if they would have to continue English-speaking careers I should have no hesitation in sending them to Columbia: if they had greater latitude of career I should send them to both Columbia and either the Sorbonne or Montpellier.... So the place of education used to seem to me immaterial and I used to be astonished at the New Yorker's unshakableness in the matter. But realizing as to-day I do how true it is that once a New Yorker you are always a New Yorker, I understand the passion better and, interested as I to-day am for

New York, I am more than contented that it should be so. And I should like to assure the reader that my interest in New York is not merely a local interest born of having had a good time in the city or of any other personal preoccupation. The really thrilling thing about New York is that she is the last chance of European civilization. For, say what you like about New York or about America, their civilizations are European, like their traditions and their blood, and if New York does not now make a good thing of it you may write: *Fuit Europa et magna gloria.* . . .

So to have at heart the cause of New York is in effect to have at heart the interests of Western humanity—of *homo Europæus sapiens*, nothing less. And one may presume that the return to New York of the children of cultured and relatively law-abiding parents is for the good of New York as, no doubt, of those children; and it is good that the city should have the power to inspire the homing instinct in its children. They do wander away—but so many return.

The old gibe against Gotham was that she was the Sink Hole of the States—a conduit through which as it were good Americans went to Paris to die . . . and bad ones to live. But the image is no longer that of a mere passageway—of a place for ever receiving accessions of populations that for ever pass on. The real fact is that the situation is one of a constant flux and reflux.

And that, as far as I am concerned, is a satisfactory position. It is not the New Yorker that renders America odious in the eyes of European populations and it is not New York that will be shocked by cultural graces learned in the Old World and brought back. And for myself what I want to see is as great a mingling as may be feasible between the peoples of such alien races as can be calculated to be of good will. Of good will! I cannot see that much good can be done to any one by a sudden influx into Europe of hordes of suddenly enriched hundred-and-twenty-per-cent Americans—but I am personally acquainted with a thousand or so of New Yorkers whose visits to those shores can only do good to themselves . . . and to Europe.

There is, I am aware, the reverse of the medal. The salvation of America I have been frequently assured can only come from the evolution by her of a solid middle class. I used to receive that assurance more frequently in the old day than at the present time; but even now I get told that about twice a day when talking such subjects. But it has long made itself manifest that in present-day conditions such a dream is the most impracticable of plans. And it grows daily more impracticable.

America is apt proudly to figure to itself that it is immune from the post-war disasters that have afflicted certain countries of Europe. But precisely the same vicissitudes have attended on America's mopping up of the gold supply of the world as have afflicted various European classes on account of their denudation of currency. The *rentier* and the intellectual classes of New York, of Brooklyn, of Hoboken . . . or of Boston, or Philadelphia and New Orleans, if their case is not yet as parlous as those of the same classes of Berlin or Paris, are beginning to find it almost as difficult to turn round as the investor and intellectual of London.

Where are the inheritors of the great American names of yesterday? There was in my day a millionaire—a "King" of something or other—who was famous not only throughout the United States but on the Boulevards and in Monte Carlo. I knew him slightly in both places and his words were listened to everywhere with that almost religious awe that used in those days to be accorded to the utterances of the unthinkably wealthy. At his death he left a sum that was then regarded as enormous —somewhere between six and ten million dollars. Well, the other day I overheard rather than heard the budget of one of his grandsons. I mean that I was at a gathering where the figures were being given not directly to myself but to a third party, I being at liberty to listen to that conversation or another as I chose. It appeared that Mr. S—— had inherited a round million dollars from his father, the son of the late multimillionaire. He estimated his unearned income from that source as fifty thousand a year. His apartment on Park Avenue cost him for rent and upkeep, servants' wages and other running expenses $13,000 per annum; alimony to two divorced wives—and he said that one could not move in his world without having at least two divorced wives—alimony then, the expenses of hospitality and his car cost him another $24,000. His car, I remember, cost him $8,000; he said that no man could run a car in New York on less. That left him $13,000 for his *menus plaisirs* . . . clothes, summer holidays, poker, racing and the like. He said that it was not enough. It was not nearly enough: he could not run a yacht and nobody of his condition could live without a yacht. So he was going to emigrate. ...

Well, $50,000 a year is just about the income that was required for a member of the English governing classes before the war ... and before the war Mr. S—— would have been quite a rich man even in America. A man quite eligible for the American governing class if America had had one. But nowadays he is nobody. So he goes.

And he is for the time at least leading a bachelor life. Imagine, then, the case of a man with a wife—only one—and a couple of children; for you cannot evolve a class without offspring for its continuance. On an unearned income of $50,000 he will be continually pressed as strained as was an English gentleman with two thousand a year before the war. He won't be able to inhabit quite the house or apartment that he would like to inhabit; at any rate, he will have to inhabit a much less spacious and dignified affair than did his parents. His wife will not have quite the dress allowances or social agreeabilities as he would like her to have; his children will have nothing like the resources that they will certainly claim as living with other children of an almost-governing class. He will experience a state of almost perpetual unease; certainly ease and he will be strangers. To remedy this he must either move to Europe or take up the chairmanship of a rubber company or other agency of sorts. In either case he will be unavailable as a member of a possible Governing Class—for these must be both resident and at leisure.

To look for a moment at a budget at the other end of the scale: I was shown one by a member of a charitable organization operating in the poorer quarters of New York. The settled income of this family was nil; they made various sums from time to time by one more or less parasitic job or another—from tips, to all intents and purposes. They were born New Yorkers on both sides of the house—one of them in particular being of a very old New England family. Well, the entire household expenses —the rent, food, clothing: at any rate the necessary clothing, the heating and the rest, were provided either by municipal and other relief or by charity. The entire, haphazard income of the family—a man, his wife, two grown sons and a nearly grown-up daughter—went to keeping up a Buick car and a wireless installation. Their view was that these last were necessities for the native-born American.

I was assured that that is by no means an uncommon case, though to what extent that is true I have naturally no means of knowing; charity workers are apt to exaggerate when generalizing and, on the other hand, the same worker assured me that the poverty and squalor of the slums of New York far exceeded those of the poorest quarters of London. I daresay that is true, for I have never, even in the narrowest underground alleys of the Mediterranean seaboard, met such horrible stenches as have assailed me in the—generally Jewish—streets of the upper Eastside of New York, whereas the Jewish quarters round the Tower and in Whitechapel are singularly cleanly. But, indeed, the streets between lower Broadway and the North River in the neighborhood of Wall Street are unsavory enough. I was watching the other day the efforts of two men and a boy with a hose to clean one of those descending roadways. I have never seen such filth as was raised by the flood of water, deposited on the sidewalk or on the passersby, and then left *in situ* by that irrigation.

And as America mops up more and more gold the prospects of the evolution of a middle-governing class must grow more and more remote with the continual fall in the value of currency. To evolve a class you must have at least a generation or two of stability and of this there seems little chance. Mind, I am not advancing the opinion that the evolution of a Middle Class *would* be a panacea for the woes of New York: I am merely commenting on a rather generally received opinion. I do not see that New York—whatever may be the case with America—I do not see that New York has any very tangible woes. Still, even as to that I am quite aware that I may easily be wrong. The conversation of the charity worker to which I have referred may well give one pause—and the consideration that the average wage of the manual and non-administrative worker of New York is said to be $28 per week. If one considers the many very much higher wages that have to come in to make up that average the lower rates of pay must be more than sufficiently exiguous. And even with twenty-eight dollars a week—and then some indeed!—I do not see myself having a good time in New York. . . . Still, that is not my affair and I do not know that I have seen anything that would lead me to think that there is any real distress in New York. . . . There are naturally the hard cases. There was one of an ex-German general who was the sort of body slave of a very unpleasant negro. . . . An utterly unhelpable case. And other unhelpables. . . . But, on the whole, the atmosphere of New York is one of hope and given that atmosphere I imagine it must be better to live on three dollars a day round about the queerly changed Bowery than on, say, four quid a week with its slightly greater purchasing power almost anywhere in London.

However, that is still not my affair any more than the Middle Classes really are. My concern in life is with Thought and the Arts and if I had to evolve a Governing Class it would be made up of a few Pure Thinkers and as many Artists as are to be found in the world. And, in New York, fluidly, you find a sufficiency of these to make up a government and, on the surface of things, they seem to do themselves well enough. Otherwise I should not here enjoy myself.

For if my brother artists are not in a position to do themselves moderately well I would rather myself starve. That is the least little cock that one can owe to Æsculapius. . . .

New York then enjoys on the surface a sufficiently vigorous artistic and intellectual life. Any one accustomed to the artistic

IT IS NOT SO MUCH THE PLACE ... 127

and thinking lives of other capitals can here feel himself perfectly at home—and perfectly normal. About the same views of the arts are held in Greenwich Village and in Chelsea and in drawing-rooms on Park Avenue as will be found in the corresponding districts in Paris. Probably on Riverside Drive—postulating for convenience that Riverside Drive is the rich-Jewish quarter—you will find more "advanced" views held than are held in average Parisian drawing-rooms—and you will find artistic or intellectual conversation anywhere in New York to be infinitely more advanced than in the most advanced attic-studios of London.

This intellectual vividness New York owes partly to the presence of an immense Jewish population, partly to the absence of a Governing Middle Class. I don't like Jews. I make the statement quite advisedly and not without tact—for, if I don't like Jews and still make the statement that the arts flourish in New York largely because of its Jewish population, the assertion may be regarded as more accurate than if I were dealing with people whom I liked and to whom in consequence I might be suspected of handing out large spoonfuls of apple-sauce. Apart from that whether I like Jews or not can be of no importance to any one.

And the fact of their artistic helpfulness is incontestable . . . at any rate as regards the plastic arts and the art of the Theatre. Jews in New York buy a great many pictures; they buy probably the greater part of the sculpture that is sold and the more recondite theatre—the less recondite also I daresay—exists solely by the suffrage, the subsidy or the attendance, of the rich or the poor Jew. The present theatrical season has not been a good one: one might indeed say that it has been pretty rotten. I at least have seen only one play that I have not been slightly ashamed of having gone to. But that is merely temporary. Two years ago I saw here more interesting plays in one month than in either London or Paris during two years and no doubt when I get forcibly taken to the play in New York this autumn the balance will again have redressed itself in favor of New York.

I don't indeed profess to be a haunter of playhouses; I never, indeed, go to one unless I am more or less forcibly taken—but that makes me a fair judge of the state of the more "advanced" theatre in any place in which I happen to be. The people who say to me: "Oh, you *must* go to So-and-So" and who take tickets and lead me to it are of a class whose enthusiasms are not roused by the theatre of commerce. Thus on the whole the *Dybbuk* in Hebrew was about the only play in New York last season that was incontestably worth being dragged to, and I was duly dragged to it by an enthusiastic young lady, not a Jewess.

That may stand as a symbol for certain sides of the artistic life of New York. There you have an amazing new art—or, if you prefer it, an amazing development of an old art; it is subsidized by richish Jews, supported amazingly by the poorer Jewish population, and produces the only play to which a young Christian enthusiast can drag an elderly and case-hardened, foreign non-enthusiast with some chance of finding her choice approved.

How it may be with literature I do not so exactly know. At any rate the only people I have found in New York—and I have not found them anywhere else at all—who really loved books with a real, passionate, yearning love that transcended their attention to all other terrestrial manifestations were Jews—and the only people who subsidized young writers during their early non-lucrative years. But rich Jews seem to do this automatically all the world over.

Rich Christians never will, though poor ones will be found to do so.

Obviously this Israelite support of the arts would not suffice in itself to make New York the art center that it is or is becoming; the majority of the support that the arts here receives is Gentile enough all right . . . but that support would hardly suffice to maintain a very vigorous artistic life in this city without the Jewish addition. It makes the difference between hardly supportable indigence and just bearable comfort.

For for a city to be an artistic—or any other—center there must be a social life for the artists or others and that social life must be of a kind to attract outsiders. Thus in New York you will find great numbers not only of resident practitioners of one or other of the arts but you will find attracted to her increasingly considerable numbers of foreigners like myself and in addition all the practitioners of the arts of other American cities which might legitimately expect to retain their artists for themselves. This is very marked indeed in the case of the art of letters.

It is strikingly the case with artistic as opposed to social life. I have boldly and impenitently asserted in my earlier pages

IT IS NOT SO MUCH THE PLACE ... 131

that for the foreigner and in a rule of thumb way, New York is the capital of the United States. But though this may be the case with financial, artistic and even, stretching the point, with administrative matters it is very impressively not so when it comes to social and other greatnesses. Nothing is indeed more impressive than the decentralization in this respect of the United States. It is not merely that the great social names of New York are practically unknown in Chicago, St. Louis, Charleston, New Orleans or Lincoln, Nebraska—not to mention California and the coast, or even Boston! There appear indeed to be no great social names in New York nowadays in the sense that twenty years ago there were the Astor and Vanderbilt families and their rather tyrannous two or three hundred of supporters. There is a very gay, insouciant and enormously expensive social life in New York but relatively few names swim to the surface of its whirlpool and those that do are for ever changing. And, on the other hand, those that do not change, those that have, as it were, names of some stability, frequent those particular parages hardly if at all.

You may sit on the dais at some sort of semipublic dinner or another say, at the Plaza Hotel—I for my sins have done it relatively often—and you will have pointed out to you a table occupied by twelve or fourteen rather dowdyish-looking people all obviously friends. And you will be told that that table represents ... my mind always boggles at these figures: say six hundred or six thousands of millions of dollars. At any rate from the impressed manner of your informant you will gather that it is something terrific and august, that sum. But you will not see those elderly, dowdyish figures at the brilliant displays of the more evanescent brilliances, though, on the other hand, you may see members of the more evanescent and brilliant crowd attending the semipublic dinners at, say, the Plaza.

In either case it seems to me—though I may well be mistaken and have little wish to dogmatize—New York offers for a city of say twelve million inhabitants singularly few names that are socially august and none at all that carry across the continent. California is said to owe the brilliant social life that it and, say, New Mexico and the Coast generally are said to possess, entirely to Eastern millionaires and that is alleged as additional proof of the nonholding power of New York. But obviously and visibly New York and more markedly Brooklyn and more markedly still Hoboken *have* settled social groups that in their very greatly varied standards of wealth are fairly cohesive and quite sufficiently old. (I get into the bad habit of using the term New York when I mean what the telephone directories call Manhattan and the Bronx. I hope I may be pardoned. For me New York is so intimately and solely the few miles of which I have so often spoken here . . . along Fifth Avenue and Broadway from the Battery!) Manhattan, then, Hoboken, Brooklyn and other regions of Greater New York have incontestably their stable, cohesive and long-established societies. You will indeed, if you search, find more old-fashionedness in any one of those *pays* than in all broad England—and I daresay you might throw in France and New England itself as make-weight. I used to know a most charming family of old maids in Stamford, Conn., and they had silhouettes of General Braddock in their parlor and went into mourning on the birthday of General Washington. That was a quarter of a century ago, but I still know to-day two families—downtown in Manhattan, not in New Orleans—who go into mourning on Lincoln's birthday; and to visit in Hoboken on Thanksgiving Day is to be thrown well back into the spacious times of Victoria. The oldest-fashioned house that I remember visiting of late years in England was that of the late Miss Braddon, a charming museum-piece that can have contained nothing more modern or less stately than the displayed objects of the Great Exhibition of the Crystal Palace in 1852. But that was modern in comparison to the house in which I was privileged to eat my Thanksgiving Dinner just lately. We had walked in dead-still autumn weather, discussing the Hall-Mills case, over the sward of a park that had once belonged to one of the families implicated in that atrocious process. Little boys and girls ran about exhibiting their faces in Guy Fawkes masks; elderly couples toddled along carrying grips and coming from the remotest parts of New Jersey or Vermont to pay their respects to still older heads of the family. And, except that those high grass levels looked down on the silver of the river and across to the silver and gray of the towering façades of the city, we might have been back in the thirties of last century, walking in Hampton Court Park and discussing the case of, say, Lady Flora Hastings.

I daresay indeed that we might have

been better thus employed for when we—
the younger son of the house, a mere stripling only a year or so older than myself—
reached the hospitable dwelling that had
been bought and built before the birth of
my friend and by his father we were still
discussing the means by which the evidence
had been obtained against the members of
that unquestionably innocent and atrociously martyred family. But we were
painedly headed off that modernity and
soon we were discussing the beauties of
Heidelberg in the sixties and revealing the
horrid and still reverberating emotions that
we had felt at first seeing a lady smoke.

We ourselves had witnessed this degradation of a sex as early as 1892, the
offenders having been Russian princesses
on a German railway; but the lady of the
house had been spared such pain for a
quarter of a century more until during that
war-work which shook so many social
canons to the base some one at a sewing-bee had produced a box of cigarettes. . . .
So Victoria reigned supreme in Hoboken;
only, after lunch in our rocking-chairs we
listened to Cornell playing Pennsylvania,
O tempora, O mores. . . .

These things tend everywhere to stratify
themselves. There is obviously in Manhat-

tan itself a sufficiency of old Knickerbocker Dutch families and of their gradually gathered Anglo-Saxon associate clans to let a chance traveler who should fall amongst them, and them only, imagine that New York is all Knickerbocker Dutch . . . at any rate all New York that counted. But the fact remains that there is no one New York Society as there is a London Society or a Tout Paris: and in New York no Cabot speaks only to Lowells, nor do New York society persons as such cut any great ice far outside Manhattan . . . and the Bronx. That the same is true of other cities in America is not so surprising, though it is surprising enough. The great names of A—— will quite astonishingly not carry any weight at all in B——, not three hundred miles away, and B—— with its really settled and quite old families ranged in their hierarchies sends absolutely no sound of its famous names to C——, D—— and F——. Obviously if you go to G—— and the report precedes you in the local press that you have once been prominent amongst the Four Hundred of New York you will be observed with more attention than if you go entirely unheralded, but in the end your social place will be assigned to you on your personal merits and relatively little because of your introductions. And this explains what at one time used to astonish me—the contentment with which people of obvious social ambitions remained in relatively quite small towns. This must seem queer to the European. France, Germany and Italy are all less centralized in this respect than is England, where if you desire to climb at all you must have an establishment not infinitely far from Park Lane—but for the Frenchman Paris certainly has an overwhelming attraction, and, although in the other countries Rome and Berlin are not the only centers, one large center or another will exercise attractions over the inhabitants of other cities only relatively smaller. But on the whole this is not the case in the United States; the attraction of dominating Country Club, the golf club, the dog shows, the race meetings and the rest of quite small cities will singularly suffice the citizens and the citizens' wives of those places, and if the result makes, sometimes rather disconcertingly to the foreigner, for Main Streetishness it does also quite remarkably make for contentment.

I suppose, in fact, that the job of making oneself known to the Society of all the

United States is one of such appalling magnitude that no one, even in the smallest of cities, is so lacking in a sense of humor as to attempt it. And American Society makes universal seasonal flittings, after Xmas to the South or to Winter sports centers, and after late Spring to centers in one or other set of Hills, so that home towns and home Main Streets are even more deserted than are Park Lane and the Quartier de l'Etoile in August. So American Society does in those resorts establish a sort of holiday hierarchy. This is founded rather on immediately disposable dollars than on home rank. The multimillionaire from Dayton, Ohio, meeting the equally—or rather more —multimillionaire from Milwaukee at Miami or elsewhere takes rank in the Social Club rather on the size and fittings of his yacht, the quantity of liquor at his disposal, the hospitality he dispenses and the like than on his standing in Dayton or Milwaukee. And in that way a sort of holiday, ready-money countyfamilydom establishes itself year by year.

In a country of such infinite millions as is the United States there will naturally be almost infinite ramifications in the way of social hierarchies. In the neighborhood of Philadelphia—to mention only conditions that I have actually observed—there are societies as close as those of any English cathedral close. And closer. Be you never so wealthy or never so intelligent you will there never get yourself called on unless you have many more credentials than would satisfy an English duchess or a bishop's lady, or be you as triple-starred in the Social Register as is the *Mona Lisa* in guides to the Louvre. And outside St. Louis there is the County, which is less penetrable and spoken of with more seriousness than was ever the case with our Shires and Dukeries. And outside Chicago there are suburbs of an almost unexampled social rigidity; and so with many other cities down to Boston.

And, of course, there is the Social Register itself. As to what this is or with how much seriousness it is taken I could never satisfy myself; nor could one of its compilers, whose acquaintance I am proud to have, ever quite make me understand. There was, for instance, a very charming and accomplished lady who was said to have come, straight from an extremely far-Western wash-tub by way of marriage and the almost simultaneous deaths and oil-striking of a husband and his partner, to a position of nearly extreme wealth. She had various social vicissitudes, so I was told, until she arrived at the position of having a golden dinner service for state occasions—though I never myself saw it. At about that time she was put upon the Social Register and, I presume, she was in future received by all other persons whose names are there found. But I could not discover from my informant—she being known to both of us—whether that really was the case; or whether she owed her advancement to the acquisition of the dinner service, to the great grace and charm of her manner, to the fact that my friend had undoubtedly what in Belgium is called a *boontje* for her as indeed I might well have had myself—or to what other cause. For the matter of that I could not discover that the lady herself felt any singular elation because of that accolade.

CHAPTER V

... AS THE PEOPLE

OF course in these matters I do not want to give myself the airs of one who dogmatizes or of a specialist. But I think that it may be accepted as a fairly safe generalization—as two fairly safe generalizations—that, firstly, New York is not the exclusive social capital of America that London is for England, Rome for Italy —or even Chicago for the Middle West. And then that New York *is* the artistic center of the Western Hemisphere. I will indeed go further and say that she is a World Center for Anglo-Saxondom.

I use the word "center" advisedly. For New York is so much more a place to which artists are attracted and from which in turn they fly than one in which they—or any one else—can dwell. The extreme closeness of social relations; the endless indulgence in social gatherings; the relative want of any privacy; the stimulus of the air as of the human type there prevalent—all these things attractive as they are make it also almost impossible there to "keep it up." So that I am open to doubt whether the actual artistic output of New York is at all formidable. Your address—your permanent *pied à terre*, may be anywhere between Greenwich and Bronx Park, but I do not think that it is here that you will work—or that here you will turn out your more permanent work. I know that I at least am giving up the attempt and that very soon it will be not from the glooms of Old Chelsea but in the blinding sunlight, beneath the bare planes of Provence that I shall be contemplating the charms of my Gotham.... Oh, with all the nostalgia in the world, I grant you. But I still want to write one good book.

No, New York is no place for the working hours of the contemplative. Obviously there are those who must stay there for long stretches: they are to be both envied and feared for. A *belle dame sans merci* has them indeed in thrall.... And I never knew whether that Man-at-Arms was the more to be felicitated or pitied—just as, asking myself the question: If you had to choose between having your vital juices sucked away by constant reclining in the arms of your Gotham—between that and never seeing her again, for which would you elect? I don't know, and fortunately for me the question hardly poses itself.

No—for me the charm of New York lies in, she is a Center because of, the immense number of human contacts that she offers you. I have pointed out that the attraction of Paris—which city I do not like—is that I seldom go out to lunch from my studio along a few yards of Boulevard without meeting some one, attractive in one way or other, with whom to consume that frugal meal. It is almost the same with New York. Indeed I here meet almost the same people. And that, in the end, is the great pleasure of life.

I have sometimes wondered whether if just the same people could gather themselves together, have *pieds à terre* in or center round some airy, sunlit city of almost perfect climate—say, Avignon!—the same pleasure would not be attained. Perhaps it might; perhaps it might not. I have tasted of something of the sort in a city on the shores of the Mediterranean and the experience was agreeable enough. One talked; one danced; one drank rosy wine. One talked; the sun shone; the wine was *rosé*, the mistral blew: one danced: one slept; the motor horns dinned like mad; one wrote; one consumed bouillabaisses; the sun shone; the sea sparkled; one wrote, one danced; one listened to Russian orchestras playing *Carmen*. . . . The company was the best in the world. . . .

But the experiment could not last. The great painters had to go to Paris—*pour la Saison Américaine;* the pull of Paris exercised itself through her publishers on the great writers; the great musicians only stayed the night and passed on; the Russian orchestra had to go to play the boatsong of the Volga at Deauville; they were replaced by an excruciating, guaranteed-English orchestra coming from Trouville. I myself had to get myself ready—with vigils over my arms —to go to New York.

And in New York I met almost the same people . . . and then some!

So that New York as a center has indeed only one rival—but that for the moment is a gigantic rival indeed—a very Goliath to a never-so-active David. For it is certain that when at last I do, by way of the Mediterranean, get to Paris I shall meet there all the people of the aforesaid Littoral city and in addition all that I met in New York and then some . . . and then some, and then some . . . and then infinitely some.

It is, however, not much more possible to work in Paris than in New York.

I do not know that that matters. The social game, gossip, the war of ideas, the exchange of technical theories and all the other things that go to make up useful artistic social life—these things are really indispensable if you are to have any vigorous artistic traditions in a city or a country. But as to whether you can pursue that social life and work at your art during the daily intervals is at least doubtful. One must recruit one's forces from humanity—but whether the operation can synchronize with that of production, again I should not like to say.

In any case the artistic life of New York is assimilating itself more and more to that of Paris—and I do not know that it does not carry the process of international fusion further than Paris allows it to be carried. The distinguished French that one begins to meet profusely on Fifth, or Park Avenues mingle with the natives, are welcomed and overwhelmed by the natives, in a way that never happens in the capital of France. There foreigners are kept rather severely at a distance—and the Middle Westerner-become-New-Yorker goes to Paris rather to meet other Middle-Westerners-become-New-Yorkers than with any hope of meeting members of the Académie

Française . . . or even of the Goncourts. And that is the slingstone of this David. It is the real slingstone. New York will achieve its position—it has achieved the position it has—rather by in- than by exclusiveness, and it is good that there should be a place where all sort of foreignesses—*all* sorts—should be united as it were in a common frame. It happens to me frequently to be told by gentlemen whose names end in "berg" or "felt" or the like that what America needs is a complete shutting of its boundaries to all Latin or English influences. I am told the same often by other gentlemen whose names begin with Mac or O'. New York, say they, must be proudly Nordic and must become completely self-centered. I also, they imply, must be excluded because I cannot be truly Anglo-Saxon since I am a "subject" not a "citizen" and true Anglo-Saxondom is all the same as true democracy. Similarly all American ports must be closed to American citizens desiring to voyage Eastwards unless perhaps they guarantee that their destination is either Berlin or Dublin. . . . That is, perhaps, not reasonable but it is at least transparent.

I used at one time to be really alarmed by these manifestations, and my alarm reached its climax when a young gentleman with a name like Mansfield told me seriously, menacingly and almost vociferously that the very strongest measures must be taken against all foreign influences in the United States. He added various other pieces of information as to the designs of American Big Business upon my Empire: within ten years Old Glory would float not only over Dublin but over Delhi, Montreal, Cape Town, Adelaide and the like. But a certain overseriousness of his tone made one realize that in effect he was speaking ironically; that he was parodying the aspirations and expressions of various captains of American industry rather than voicing his own ideals or those of any normal Americans.

I must obviously return to that side of matters, but for the moment I will stick to my text, which is that it is a good thing for the world that New York exists and is a meeting-place for good brains. And that it does unite them as it were in a sort of a *cadre* . . . as if all sorts of different sizes and designs of type were being pressed and held together in one printer's frame.

It is a good thing that I who am about as English as they make them can, as I have already pointed out, sit at table with a dozen other persons all to me foreigners in a foreign city and feel entirely ordinary and at home—much more ordinary and much more at home than I should feel at any London table—or at any other table outside Provence itself! But it is a still better thing that that can happen to members of dozens and dozens of other races all more type-hardened and as it were more insular. For in that way New York assumes more and more the aspect of being the birthplace of humanity.

And it becomes hourly more necessary that that is what we should see—and soon! . . . for the breathing space allowed to European-derived civilization is not infinite. No Empire and no Republic can very much longer afford to carry on in a spirit of uncabined hundred percentism and the world cannot support the appearance of another power having an aspect of Prussianism. From this aspect of bogeydom New York redeems its country—and it redeems its country far more by the cordiality it displays to cosmopolitan artists and thinkers than by the fact that it is the financial center of the Western Hemisphere. It is perhaps bad *per se* that in New York Erse and Teutons should have unbridled opportunity to voice indirectly the wrongs of

Kathleen ni Houlihan or the reverses of Essen-manufactured arms . . . but it is better that they should have liberty to raise their voices than that hospitality should not be universal.

The modern world suffers so much from facilities of transport that it would be sad indeed if facility of transport did not do something to redress *that* balance by mingling the more tolerant and reasonable of men. Almost infinite harm is done by the swift carriage of newly enriched hooligans from Wigan or the suburbs of Birmingham and the too cheap transport of continually impoverished old maids from Leamington or Putney—all in England—into foreign parts. And even greater harm is done by the export of enriched hundred-per-centers and the ram-faced, silver-haired and be-spectacled female autocrats of Main Streets from all the North American half-continent into Europe. And not much good is done by the rarer visits of inspecting Europeans to the United States.

But the artist and the thinker are as a rule more tolerant and never having enjoyed any great comforts in life or any assurance of them they will put up with quite a good deal in the way of international strangenesses. Take celery. . . . It is monstrous to eat blanched celery with olives as an *hors d'œuvre*. For God surely meant celery to be eaten along with Stilton cheese at the end of a full meal, just before the port. . . . Yet in New York—*horresco referens*—blanched celery is continually eaten as I have described. I may add that in Paris the idea of eating celery raw at all causes a shudder to run down the French spine. The French God meant celery to be eaten in soup, or braised or what is called *demi glacée*.

Now at a New York club in company with three Englishmen engaged on or about the purlieus of literature and two Frenchmen, one a portrait painter and the other a sculptor, I have contentedly munched celery before anything else . . . and so did all my company. And they never spoke a mumbling word. . . . On the other hand at the hospitable board of a magnate—not in New York—I listened to the patronizing harangue of a British magnate who had come over to inspect American methods in his own line of business. He told our host that in God's Own Country Eng., not God's Own Country U. S. A., celery always closed a meal with the Stilton. He said that every man who knew what was what always closed his meals with celery and Stilton; he said that if you really knew the cleansing effect of celery eaten with Stilton cheese when it came to the subsequent slow degustation of real old English port you would never eat anything else. He said that only such hardly educated persons as the inhabitants of States symbolized by abbreviations like "Mo." and "Ill." would ever think of eating celery except after a meal; then it should be accompanied by Stilton cheese and washed down by a good glass of old Port. A good glass of old Port from a good old English cellar, as only the half educated did not know, was infinitely enhanced by the cleansing action of celery and Stilton—ripe old English Stilton—eaten together at the end of a meal. . . . Why our hostess did not smack his face I could not imagine. It was all I could do not to. . . .

Well, it would have been better if Sir John had not come to America. For, somewhere in the neighborhood of a place in God's Own Country Eng. where they manufacture small arms or something of the sort he is still burbling about when celery should or should not be eaten. And his family, assembled about him are exclaiming: "Great Scott! They eat *celery* at the beginning of lunch. . . . Oh I say, just listen to what the dad says. . . . They eat celery . . . *celery*, mind you . . ." And the information is conveyed to the more imbecile of English journals. And there is no end to it. . . .

I should like to know what proportion of the responsibility for the Napoleonic wars and for the War to End War respectively should be assigned to the fact that one Enemy Nation ate sausages and the other the legs of frogs. . . . Yet they eat ten times as many frogs in New York alone as in all France and as much Frankfort sausage in Chicago and New York together as in all High Germany.

About internecine and international Kitchens—but more particularly about the Oyster as a symbol of differences between nations—I am going to have my say almost immediately. Let me now wind up my utterances as to the cosmopolitanism of Gotham.

I am tempted to revoice some one's epigram to the effect that New York is the art center of Anglo-Saxondom because New York is not London. And that is fairly true. It is fairly true really because to be an art center a city must offer some sort of social *agréments* to artists. You might think that you could perfectly well have a city that was an art center solely because it contained consumers of art products, those troublesome people, the producers, being kept severely at a distance. But you never *do* have such a condition of things, I do not know why. Even in the eighteenth century of Sir Joshua Reynolds when Dukes of Norfolk and the like were always sitting for their portraits and going on Grand Tours for the purpose of studying the arts you found that the portrait painters got invited to dinners of the Kit Cat Club and the like. And that was as near as London ever came to being a city of the Arts.

To have a social life depends not so much —depends hardly at all—on great stored-up or great diffused wealth; it depends solely on having enough families of identical or almost identical resources to occupy the leisure times of the participants in that society. French literary life to-day must be about as impecunious an affair as the world has ever seen; so with French military, naval, judicial and all other forms of avocational life. These people live on almost nothing and to them the $28 a week of the New York manual laborer would be almost affluence. Yet their social lives are crowded, animated, gay—in a word sufficient; and their professional lives are cheerful, honorable, efficient and dignify their great nation.

You can just say as much of the artistic

life of New York to-day—of the artistic life of New York plus that of the Paris-American colony you can say it without reservation. A writer or painter with a *pied à terre* in either Paris or New York and with easily found accommodation in either New York or Paris can do himself very well indeed—I mean socially and intellectually. On the other hand, I do not believe that any writer of much seriousness of artistic purpose could live continuously in New York, whilst it may be true—though I doubt it—that a writer living continuously in Paris will lose touch with American conditions. He might very probably lose touch with American markets—but in that I am not interested.

You may say that all this is no affair of mine—but I get asked so continuously questions on this subject by private persons and public organs that I suppose what I have to say about it may be of some interest. I happen to have had lately—and indeed continue to have—opportunities for knowing where and how American works are produced—more opportunities than are possessed by nearly all American laymen and, I daresay, than many persons actively engaged in the publication of books in the United States. And I may add that if I had not had a certain enthusiasm for American literature I should not have put myself in the way of encountering those opportunities.

There arises sporadically and from time to time in American literary circles a sort of patriotic fervor which is not so much a Xenophobia as a sort of determination that all matter printed in America shall be marked: *Written and manufactured in the United States.* I should have really nothing to say against that if the ideal were possible of realization and unlikely to interfere with literature in general. Before, however, it can be realized, the promoters must ensure that living and social conditions in New York are such that American literature can there be produced. And nowadays those conditions are just not good enough. At the prices paid to quite prominent practitioners of the Arts you cannot there get tranquillity enough, social ease enough—and above all you cannot get household service enough to provide you with interesting food, and completely smooth domestic conditions.

I do not mean to say that all these things are necessary adjuncts of the lives of all artists—but they are the indispensable conditions for so many that where they are absent, either the average level of artistic output must fall or the workers *must* go elsewhere. They *must* go elsewhere. . . . And it is to be remembered that I have spoken only of the more promient artists—of those with so assured a market that they can at any rate to some extent dictate their own prices. But a man must have worked long before he will have attained to such conditions—and to have worked long in an atmosphere so exacting and amongst vicissitudes so sudden and disastrous as pertain in American cities is to have run rather terrible risks. . . . Rather terrible risks both mental and hygienic.

Living conditions in New York—and I presume elsewhere in America—are so terribly costly that almost the only resort of the young artist there if he has to make a living is one form or other of journalism or of commercial art. The aspirant thus hopes to make bread and butter whilst throwing off this or that piece of imaginative work. One day, one or other of those pieces will "catch on" to one or other of the mysterious cogs of the immense machine that makes for fortunes for the Imaginative. One prays that it may.

But the enterprise is very desperate. . . . In New York it is too desperate. Journalism and the commercial arts may be the most admirable sticks but they are terribly exacting mistresses. And they are all the more exacting in that they have excitements of their own. It is probably almost as—or it is on occasion almost more—exciting to have brought off a great journalistic scoop or to have attained to super-eminence in the realm of advertisement, strip-picture, or magazine-cover designing as to have arrived at slow fame by any amount of imaginative-artistic achievement. The glories and emoluments are more immediate and more obvious and the performances less exacting.

But, even if the journalist make no scoop to draw him away from his more imaginative ambitions and the commercial artist no entry into a Tom Tiddler's ground where he may for ever remain, the mere occupation of making a living by daily tasks is desperately hard and engrossing. Yet to think out works of art takes time.

There is a belief that seems to me to be very prevalent in America at this moment that journalism is a good road to imaginative achievement because it brings you into contact with Life. At any rate lately in Chicago I was appalled by an early-morning invasion of my bedroom. The day before, in the course of an interview, I had happened to say incautiously that journalism was an avocation exactly opposed to that of producing works of fictional art. And the young men and women who burst in on my—quite early—slumbers and who continued to burst in on my occupations during most of that and several successive days were all students at one or other Journalists' College in one or other of the Universities of the Middle and Northwest.

"How is this?" they would all exclaim, in effect. "You say that Journalism is bad for Novel Writing. But we are all taking courses of from three to five years in Journalism in order to become Novelists . . ." or essayists, or poets in either strict verse or *vers libre*.

I would withdraw into nonself-committal stammerings. I pointed out that what I had said to my interviewer of yesterday had really been this.: I did not know much about the matter but I was pretty certain that the qualities that made a man a good novelist would make him a bad journalist and so I considered it a corollary that the qualities that made a man a good journalist would make him a bad novelist. Or rather, to reduce the matter to its lowest denominator. I might or might not be a good novelist; I had no means of knowing; but I was certain that I should make a damn bad journalist because I could not write short. I needed space in which to develop my ideas ... several or many paragraphs. I could not run to "snap." No can do.

They, taking no interest in my predicaments since they were so immersed in their own, would counter with the allegation that their professors and other pastors and masters assured them that the career of a journalist was of the greatest use to the imaginative writer because it brought him into contact with Life. They visited murderer's female companions in their homes; they saw conflagrations destroy elevators; they detected crime; they interviewed the distinguished and the villainous; they had exceptional opportunities of knowing how unusual things were done. So they saw Life.

That let me out and with animation I pointed out that that was not seeing life. The newspaper of necessity presented you with a distorted image of life simply because it had to be more interesting than life. If I judged Life by the Chicago newspapers I must think the world gone mad. Yet life in Chicago was perfectly normal. The journalist had to tell you that he smelt the Stockhouses in the foyer of Chicago Opera

House. But you did not. Neither did he. I said that the way to see life was to live, but the journalist did not live. At any rate he did not live the life that he wrote about. He rushed feverishly about with his eyes and ears unnaturally open. But even murderers sometimes sit quietly at home, reposing with their arms round their female companions, drinking near beer. For most of the time. . . .

Then those young men and women in my bedroom would say that they did not take much stock in my opinion, but they liked to hear all sides.

Nevertheless there is a great deal in what I say. The way in which to gather knowledge of life for the purpose of conveying through your writings the image of life itself—the only way *is* to live. And if possible to live before you write. If I had a son I should want him to write imaginative work; there is no better or more dignified occupation. But before he did so, I should recommend, he should earn his living—as a sailor, an agricultural laborer, a veterinary surgeon—as anything that was real and non-parasitic. I would even let him be a Financier or a Big Business Man if nothing else would serve the turn. To me at least it seems to be merely common sense to say that as the stuff of poetry is the industries, vicissitudes, fears, emotions, sufferings and passions of normal humanity, the writer will write better about these things if he has really experienced them than if he has only looked on at their more extreme manifestations.

But there are always uncommon cases to which common sense rules will not apply. There must be young men and women, of genius even, who are unsuited to gain their early livings at normal occupations, or whose feelings will not let them do so. For these New York is the best place in America . . . but it is not a good place because it does not arrange itself to suit their necessities. Until it does so it must be content to see such young men and women drift . . . into expatriation.

For them there is . . . Paris. And there might be very much worse places. For Paris has long since adapted herself to affording easy and dignified living conditions for very poor artists, and the formula for the young man or woman of some genius coming from remoter America is very simple and very stereotyped. He or she will visit New York, find living conditions there so hard as to be impossible; will make just enough money to get to Paris and to stay there; will there produce as saleable work as he or she can; will revisit New York as often as Finance will permit and will eventually find such recompense as Fate is determined to allow to him or her.

I will now recount the history of my only *faux pas* in New York . . . at any rate of the only one of which I am conscious. It has a double moral.

I was sitting then, late one evening, very fatiguedly, deep in an armchair in a hospitable, darkened, rather book-lined room that might have been Bloomsbury, or Hampstead or Oxford. I had been invited to meet some one who at the moment was only two hours late. We had dined almost too well; the wine had been. . . . But one does not talk about that.

There was at any rate conversation going on. A very distinguished critic, a more than distinguished collector, some one else as distinguished and some one else almost more distinguished. And as became the book-lined dim room the conversation was about Poetry—and I did not join in. I mean that the conversation concerned itself with a sort of poetry about which I do not talk—by a foreign poet who is an admirable fellow. And I have long considered that dog should not eat dog.

The conversation went on and on. I was thinking about American cooking, a subject that was then no little concerning me ... I mean from the moral side. I was thinking with some terror that on the morrow I was leaving my charmed circle, and going into New England where on the next morning but one I should eat for breakfast: oysters, grilled sausages with pancakes and maple syrup and an enormous slab of mince-pie. (It is no good telling me that they do not eat oysters and mince-pie for breakfast in New England. I have too often seen them do it—and done it.) I was considering that such a breakfast would be good for one—was *meant* for one—in the days when one afterwards went up into the blinding mists of the mountains and hewed timber, or over the turnips with the dogs after partridge. But nowadays one should eschew both New England and old English cookery. That I was dreamily thinking whilst the conversation went on over my nearly prostrate frame.

On and on. And on. About the same foreign poet. I was considering the elaboration of a lazy theory to the effect that if the American—*not* the New York—character had its unamiable sides it must come from diet. Pie and cereals. ... Above all cereals. Or perhaps above all pie . . . were calculated to make one grow in a virtue of a terribly hundred-per-cent disagreeableness. I began figuring out a diet-campaign that might make the Middle ·West a hundred-per-cent human. Of Boston one might well despair . . . then into my reflections came the voice of one asking me— *ME*—if I had not printed the first poem of the poet they were minutely discussing. A most admirable fellow, I said that—that he was a most admirable fellow. An assemblage of all the manly virtues. But I did not think I had had that privilege.

The voice of the great Collector insisted that I had. He possessed the files of some periodical or other that had once belonged to me. I did not insist. Dog after all should not eat dog. . . . They went on discussing the works of that poet. On and on. And on.

I became conscious of a slight headache; a slight feeling of nervous irritation. It was due either to the dinner we had eaten or to the thought of the breakfast I was to eat on the morrow after next. I grew warmer and more somnolent and as I grew more somnolent I resented more and more that conversation. It seemed to me an outrage; one does not come to New York to hear that sort of thing. And I was leaving New York. I hated leaving New York and going to . . . what was it Herrick called it? The dull confines of the drooping. . . . Oh, well, New England. . . . And suddenly I heard my voice burst out:

"For God's sake can't you fellows give over talking about the imbecile mud of that imbecile ass and talk about a decent American poet?"

Dog alas, had eaten dog. . . . I have never ceased regretting the outburst. But its immediate results were overwhelming. A complete silence descended in which you could hear the deep breathings of my fellow guests. It was like being in French Flanders where I had once heard single shells falling into a church and the thin sifting sound of the stained glass as after each explosion showers of it tinkled down into the roofless chancel. Then the awed voice of the collector said:

"But haven't Her Majesty Queen Victoria, the Captain of the Marylebone Cricket Club, the Dean of Westminster, the Head Waiter at Hurlingham and the Committee of the Carlton Club all certified that he is a poet and gentleman after their own hearts."

I was by that recovering myself. I said: "Indeed, yes. Not one of the best of the second best London clubs should be without him. . . . But why not talk about the poems of Mr. Arlington Robinson, who is a poet of the same genre but a million times better?"

(It was in effect Mr. Arlington Robinson for whom I had been waiting, by then nearly two hours and a half.)

You should have heard them sigh with relief. You see, they did not like talking about that foreign poet's work; they had been doing it to make me, a foreigner, feel at home. So that they were at once gratified to be able to leave off doing it and relieved to have my testimony as to the poet's eligibility for good clubs. And indeed he was an admirable fellow.

So we talked for a time about Mr. Robinson—who did not turn up; and then someone quoted quite a lot of Shelley's *West Wind* and soon we were singing: "He was a man, he was doing her wrong!" and other folk-songs. I like the way New Yorkers—and inhabitants of Boston too, for I have heard them do it at the Boston equivalent of the London Athenæum Club—I like the way then that New Yorkers sing after their dinners. Three or four young men get together in a corner of a room and set up a college song in four parts; then two or three others simultaneously start a dialect ballad;

others sitting on the floors in other rooms begin to sing *Ich grolle nicht* or *Ich weiss nicht was soll es bedeuten* and from a special combination of wireless and gramophone a dark, enormous voice peals out in *Deep River*. ... It is so exactly what the occupants of Oxford Common Rooms or members of the Athenæum do not do after dinner; and as my life has been spent in avoiding doing what those gentlemen do do, I like what here I find.

But the absence of the academic element in New York society does make life bitter hard all America over for a certain class of literary talent. ... America's mopping up of the world's gold supply keeps even its more distinguished imaginative writers and nonreporting journalists always under a threat of straitened circumstances. The emoluments of the pen are the last of honoraria to rise in sympathy with the fall in the purchasing value of currency and it is only lately even in America that literary earnings have in any way jumped with the jumping prices of all commodities and services. Every American working man possesses and has long possessed an automobile —but I know many, many American men of letters who do not and most of those who do have only lately acquired them.

Now I am far from saying that the possession of an automobile implies anything much in the way of rational happiness to its possessor, indeed I should say that it did nothing of the sort, and that as opposed to the American working man, the English and still more the French working man had far more opportunity for happiness—supposing that his ingredients of happiness were in any way the same as mine, which last is naturally the determining factor. But the possession of a resource by a class is at least a barometric indication of pecuniary levels when it is pointed out that another class does not as a rule run to that resource. And it is hardly an exaggeration to say that the rise in the rate of emoluments in the learned classes of America has nothing like kept pace *pro rata* with the enormous rise that has come to the classes making a living by manual labor and by the superintendence of manual laborers. . . . But, indeed, happening to visit an engineering works where I had a friend who possessed quite remarkable scientific degrees and attainments and who worked partly on investigation in the laboratories and partly actually at the furnaces . . . happening, then, to ask this young man what he was paid, I was told a sum that I have forgotten but that seemed relatively very minute—and I was begged not to reveal what that sum was anywhere because if the laborers amongst whom he part-worked should get to know how little he was paid, they would lose all respect for him and he would have his life made burdensome.

It is seldom that one finds such direct evidence that the possession of theoretic knowledge of a trade or mystery is a disadvantage from the point of view of salary—but such cases are by no means rare and grow daily more numerous. And again, I do not mean to say that even rate of pay as long as it is of a nature to keep body and soul together need have anything to do with happiness or decency of life. During several periods of my career I must have worked for far less money than any compositor to-day in either London or New York and I am quite certain that those periods were by no means the least dignified or socially agreeable that I have known.

But a rise in prices of commodities means something more—and more disastrous—than mere fall in wages; it means the gradual squeezing out and disappearance of whole trades—and more particularly what are called luxury trades. Then their providers must starve. And that is what has happened to the more learned, standardized and aloof forms of the art of criticism in America to-day. It has happened indeed to the art of poetry—but poetry has always been in that position; only until latterly the poet in America has as a rule managed to struggle along with the help of payments for writing critical articles. Now that resource has completely or almost completely gone.

I do not mean that I set any great store by the ponderous and usually almost completely imbecile "Review" which is such a feature of the printed matter of my own country, or for the daily and weekly journals where the same sort of stuff, slightly watered down, is offered to—and avoided by—the public. Indeed the greatest part of my life has been spent in combating those indolent pomposities. The existence of such sorts of printed matter and their acceptance at the hands of the public as representing Criticism is mostly responsible for the fact that the English as a nation hardly read at all. The public says, that is to say: If the books that these writers praise are indeed good books we don't like them; on the other hand, we do not want to read bad books which might be bad for us. Let us go and see a football match. . . . So it becomes increasingly difficult for any young, lively or aggressive talent in England to find any opening at all.

And the lively and agreeable way in which books and the arts generally are treated in the lighter American periodicals is, *pari passu*, responsible for the extraordinary—the extraordinary!—vividness, curiosity and life that are exhibited by the American public with regard to those subjects. I do not know that I am a writer of any merit; no one has any means of knowing that with regard to himself; but whatever my merit, it is equal in Great Britain and the United States. . . . And to be a writer in England is to be like—oh, say, a tin of jellied eels that has for years reposed on a country grocer's shelves—whereas if you were a piece of bread on a mill-pond that contained a hundred thousand hungry minnows you would not be one-tenth so pulled about as if you were a writer of any position at all in New York. . . . And as to America!

It is of course, partly a social matter—but it is very largely one of publicity. Let us put it that in England there are titles and the English can therefore display, as to the habits and ideas of titled people all that lively curiosity that they do not display for artists and their products. The place of the titled in America is filled—and quite admirably filled—by the millionaire; but the millionaire—and indeed even the billionaire have not quite the divine right to public curiosity that pertains to a wholesale fishmonger who shall have received the accolade of his Sovereign. Not *quite!* And their habits are perhaps not so picturesque. I don't know. I imagine that if you have an aristocracy it can afford time to be bad—bold and bad; whereas Big Business is a more strenuous affair. And then Big Business Men have to be so surrounded by detectives that it must be difficult to be picturesque and practically impossible to be naughtily so. At any rate all the personal pronouncements of the really Big Business Man that I have come across have been of an astonishingly virtuous hue. I cannot imagine, say, the Duke of Westminster writing like Mr. Henry Ford, whose works I have read with a singular sense of improvement. I have never seen either the Duke or my distinguished namesake—nor for the matter of that have I ever seen a portrait of either; but I imagine that the Duke and his usual associates would be more likely to occupy space on the shiny pages of social periodicals than Mr. Ford and his. . . . Those pages must, however, be filled; editors and public are alike hungry for stuff that will fill them. So the Artist has to be called in. . . . And I imagine that my friend Mr. Dreiser and Mr. Ford between them get about as much publicity as the Duke in England off his own bat. . . . But I hope Mr. Dreiser gets much, much more.

All that is very much for the good of the arts and of the world. For although it is the work rather than the personality of the artist that is of value, where a great deal of curiosity is satisfied as to the personality of the artist some attention at least will be paid to his work. And the press that pays that attention will at least try to be readable.

That then is all to the good. You have, in New York at least, no governing Middle Class, that class being everywhere the enemy of the artist, but you do have a sort of gay, changing and artistically harmless Smart Set that has neither the morgue of entrenched academic classes nor the enforced exclusiveness of ancient aristocracies. On the contrary, the New York and even the American, rich and newly enriched, are apt to see that a certain prominence, even a certain historic durability of name, sometimes come from contact, or even association, with the Great Artist. . . . There was, for instance, a Philip of Spain who is immortal because he picked up the dropped paint-brush of Velasquez. I do not know what else he did. He was perhaps the non-productive husband of Mary II (Bloody) of England and perhaps he launched a thousand ships upon which God blew so that they were destroyed. . . . *Afflavit Deus et dissipati sunt.* . . . I do not know about that. But I do know that one of the most monumentally active and wealthy men of New York, a man so active that you have to enter his house by a secret door after sitting for an examination by detectives, for all the world as if you were being measured for the Bertillon system—and of activities so formidable that he has had to be put in commission as it were by the United States Government . . . this gentleman then remarked to me that he always liked to be in the society of the late Messrs. Abbey and Sargent because Philip of Spain was famous for having picked up the paint-brushes of the Sargent of his day. And when I asked him which Philip that was he said he did not know and did not care. And neither did I.

I have indeed heard that on the days on which the best known portrait-painter in New York to-day keeps open house in his studio there will be six hundred, or it may be six thousand, million dollars there represented at tea-time. And his studio when *he* drops a brush resembles the scene on the field when Princeton plays football with Harvard. . . . That is no doubt an exaggeration. Still a certain parallel could be drawn between the Athens of the days of Pericles and to-day's New York. Pericles had mopped up all the silver in the world and all the artists in the world very naturally followed it to Athens and were awarded escorts of drums and fifes. It is true that Athens soon fell upon disaster. So, coincidentally did Spain shortly after she had mopped up all the gold of the then world and Philip honored the painter. For it would seem to be a rule of Nature that a race cannot mop up the world supply of either precious metal and afterwards prosper. In revenge it will take to honoring the arts.

Be that as it may there can be no doubt that the increase of the gold at the disposal of the United States has caused prices to harden and that the hardening of prices has caused the disappearance of the more ponderous forms of American critico-literary periodicals. At the same time the increasing esteem in which New York and America hold the arts is having the effect of enormously increasing the number of their practitioners in those countries. Nothing is indeed so striking as the increase of attendances at the already very numerous universities and colleges that cover the United States. You see old colleges that for years have gone on with from four to five hundred undergraduates suddenly, in the course of a twelvemonth, being attended by from fifteen hundred to two thousand, and the greater State Universities, like those of California, growing to numbers that are almost incredible. . . . Of course nothing like all these students address their studies to the humanities, but the numbers of those taking what is called "English" as a course must have quintupled itself in the last twenty years, whilst if you add to that the number that enroll themselves in the classes for Journalists, the increase must be still more sensational. And all these students, young men and women, must contemplate more or less seriously producing works of the pen or the typewriter in their after years. And another curious factor is the relatively new disposition of the American parent to regard the Arts as offering dignified and moderately lucrative careers to their offspring.

In the old days the American father relentlessly cut off with a shilling any son of his who proposed to become any sort of an artist, the mothers weepingly acquiescing the while. Of course that still happens, but the number of American fathers who to-day accept such a position with equanimity or even with complacency must have very sensibly increased and, as for the mothers . . . although I am constantly being asked questions by them as to whether or no Paris is a good place to which to let one's son go in order to study the arts I do not think that I have once been asked lately whether one sort of artistic career or another was or was not a good thing for a young man or woman.

The net result of all this unparalleled artistic activity—unparalleled at any rate for Anglo-Saxondom—is that a very great number of young things with only very slender talents behind their enthusiasms become artists; and that in addition the number of young things of quite considerable artistic but almost completely unmarketable gifts is also steadily on the increase. It is these last that to-day suffer very severely.

They suffer very severely because the heavier type of periodical never had any great vogue in the United States and has now a very much diminished one, so that the state of the young—or even the old—writer whose gift lies towards what in England is called Belles Lettres—towards the essay, the critical article and the poem—is apt to be very dreadful indeed. For it is to be remembered that, heavy and pompous as the great monthlies and quarterlies usually were, they sometimes belied themselves by publishing something delicate and good. The hours of depression that I have passed in New York—and there have of course been some—have arisen very largely from that set of causes. It is dreadful to see young persons of great if tenuous gifts want not only the most indispensable comforts of life but any visible or imaginable means of securing the barest recognition. And of that there is too much in New York.

It is a state that will no doubt one day cure itself. The taste for the larger canvas and the more vivid hues of popular work—I am not casting any stones at the more popular type of work; heaven forbid that I should. The most vulgar excesses of the most popular press are better for the nation, for humanity and even for the arts than the least deleterious of pompous scholasticisms —but the taste for the exclusively vivid is apt to sate itself in the natural course of things. Then comes the day of more delicate arts. That is really all that there is to be said or to hope for. In the meantime that type of American talent can only say: Thank God for Paris.

And that type of hundred-per-cent or Teuto-Erse American who clamors against the expatriate artist is doing a very cruel thing . . . and a very unpatriotic. People of delicate talent are as necessary to national life as the most blatant of successful industrialists—as necessary as the priest. Otherwise your nation becomes a howling pandemonium. And if you cannot, for temporary economic reasons, keep them alive within the walls of your own city you must let them found colonies outside. For the prosperous and the alert New York is a very beautiful place. It is as I have said again and again, outside Provence, the most beautiful place that I know. They are complement and supplement, those two.

But only if you are fortunate . . . or resilient. Meager means and closed opportunities on the other hand, there, are terrible and not to be supported. Even dead poverty with accompanying relief are better. The poor are on the whole well cared for; there is much bread distributed and many free circuses. It is pretty in the dark days of winter to see the Xmas trees beneath

Washington Square Arch or on Madison Square. I do not know that the like is to be seen anywhere else at any time. But the struggle to keep the head above water in New York is worse than is the case in any other region that I know. And the reason does not lie in the worship of wealth. London is a rather nasty place in which to be poor because the nature of my countrymen is such as to accord no human respect to the man who cannot afford a considerable establishment—preferably without working to support it. You might there be Darwin, Descartes, Ronsard and Apelles rolled into one but if you did not live at a good address you would not have the respect of your neighbors or any recognition from the wives of bishops. And that is galling. Otherwise one can scrape along on relatively little in London. . . . And Paris is the best place in the world in which to be poor because it is a city arranged for the life of the poor; there if you have wealth you are suspect whilst if you are known to be a poet the gens d'armes stop the traffic for your crossing and the commanders of state fortresses turn out the guard in your honor. That is agreeable, but one can get on without it.

But New York is terrible not because of

the snobbishness of its inhabitants; there is next to no snobbishness there. On the whole you will there be very little looked down on for being poor and indeed I believe that a millionaire in America—and even in New York—will have a worse chance before a jury than any gunman who is penniless. That is always agreeable and I daresay that if there were any garrison in New York its commander would turn out its guard to meet a distinguished poet if the proceeding were suggested to him and he thought it would give pleasure. . . . No, if you are poor in New York no one will much trouble you. You will have to go without. And there, that is terrible.

It is terrible with a terribleness passing nearly all others, not because you will have to do without luxuries or the glorious habiliments of the more fortunate. We can all do without those. . . . No, it is terrible to be poor in New York, terrible for the contemplative, because of the extreme dearness of all personal service.

The thinker—and every artist in the end is chiefly a thinker—is the bare and naked thing he is before the wind of circumstance chiefly because of his dependence on personal assistance and surveillance. Every incidental attention that he has imperiously to pay to his material surroundings is an interruption to a train of thought. I do not say that a poet may not with advantage to himself spend hours a day in digging in his garden, but the constant train of petty interruptions of domestic life will as often as not completely destroy his thought. He must then either get outside help or live in squalor upon dreadful food.

I am not saying anything against the quality of domestic help in New York or even in America. Such domestic help as you do get is admirable in its considerateness and its efficiency and so indeed is the public and semipublic service when it comes in contact with the individual. You will not find anywhere in the world better service than you will get from Pullman porters, hotel valets, parlormaids and the like. Of course you will get as good from attached retainers in Europe, but you will not get much better. I imagine that two things contribute to this—the fact that negroes set the pace in personal public services, so that such white attendants on the public as you find are forced self-protectively to adopt the touching airs of personal affection as still distinguish the Southern born negro. And then, presumably, such Europe-born domestic servants as one finds in New York and elsewhere are domestic servants by avocation. Otherwise with all the opportunities that Big Business offers them in its workshops, they would do something else. . . . At any rate where service is to be found it is of a very admirable quality whether in public caravansaries or in the homes of the rich and the moderately rich—of a very admirable quality, engrossed in its occupation and very agreeable and soft to receive. And not servile.

That I suppose is again the negroid touch —the negroid contagion. For me there is nothing so disagreeable as to be waited on by European men-servants. I have always the feeling that your English butler or Italian waiter with their differing obsequiousnesses have in the backs of their minds the ambition to revenge themselves eventually on you either by blackmail or the knife —and I do not know that the English house-parlormaid is much better. I shiver not infrequently whilst she hovers round me. But the negro servant is cheerful, self-assertive, interested—and singularly soft in his or her ministrations. And I think, as I have already said, that the white domestic staff is apt to take its color by degrees from the negro just as, it seems to me, all real American cooking has its coloring from the admirable concoctions of the Southern negress. . . . And of course there is American music!

But the pity of it is that there is not enough of it to go round or nearly round; and to live in America—and still more in New York—to live at all, you have, unless you are at least moderately rich, to subsist on standardized and devitalized food, without personal attention, in an atmosphere either of very dreadful public meals and domesticities or of continual personal stress. For even if you eat off paper plates nothing that has not come out of a tin, if your heating be entirely central and all your domestic work done with the aid of labor-saving appliances, the domestic work of even a very small establishment will be fairly exhausting if you have other work to think about. And all the while your vitality will be suffering because of the quality of your sustenance and your want of personal ease. . . . It is all the bliss of life to have some one fetch a handkerchief for you.

I had a deep glimpse into this the other day. I was talking to the wife of a very admirable poet and critic somewhere downtown—precisely on these subjects. And I was unfolding theories of food which I shall presently unfold here at some length. . . .

I do not, by the bye, apologize for treating in these pages of subjects that are usually considered to be beneath the attention of the Muse. These things are the stuff of life . . . of national life as opposed to national glories. It is no doubt very glorious that one man in a great nation should have at his disposal one billion dollars. I am really not in the least ironical. I remember the wave of emotion that went over the United States when we read in the morning papers that one man possessed a billion dollars. . . . That was the sort of people we were: we had produced a man who possessed a billion dollars. No doubt the same sort of wave of emotion went over Hellas when the Hellenes read in their morning papers that Herakles had cleansed the stables of Augeas. They were the sort of people who produced demi-gods.

But life is made up of the people who creep up and down between those mighty legs . . . not of demi-gods. So rather than write of the possessor of a billion as typefying New York I prefer to write of things culinary. . . . Thus I was talking to the wife of a very admirable poet and critic, somewhere downtown . . . about cooking. I will not here enlarge upon my theories. Roughly speaking I said that people leading a town existence did not need to be crammed with cereals as a Dorking fowl is crammed with mash by the higgler. Obviously if you lift heavy weights or dig in heavy soil you will lose weight yourself and that loss must be supplied. But the poet-critic sits in a chair from dawn till eve. It is his brain that needs support. Between seven A. M. and eleven P. M. he will not have lost half an ounce. . . . So if you make him spend an hour and a half in chewing dried wheat you will not have supplied him with anything but fat-reparative material, his brain will starve and his time be wasted. . . . What you must give him is several portions of different fish and non-refrigerated meat, cooked with extraordinary care, seasoned, deep-fried, parboiled, baked, cooled-off and rebaked with the sauces from the bones and fat, strained and added at the last moment as a marinade. So he will obtain the fuel that his brain needs.

There went up at my words an extraordinary wail from the wife of that poet-critic. . . . This is a true tragedy told lightly. She said:

"For heaven's sake do not let Harry hear what you are saying. I love him. He is much, *much* too thin. . . . But how can I feed him as you say? . . . I work all the morning as secretary to an advertisement-writer and all afternoon as a mannequin on Third Avenue. . . . So I tell him that what he really needs is cereals . . . vitamins No. 13 and 14 with a proper balance of proteins and calories. . . . I don't know what it means. . . . It probably means, poor dear, that he ought sometimes to have what he likes to eat. . . . I do not mean that that is what the advertisement writers mean, but that that is what his thinness and his dreadful, dreadful appetite mean!"

CHAPTER VI

THE LORDLY DISH

I SELDOM sit down to an American meal without remembering pleasurably the scriptural verse: "He asked for water and she gave him milk; she brought forth butter in a lordly dish," and when I am not otherwise engaged I frequently wonder why it is that Americans who are not sparing of their criticisms of things Continental never—or never as far as I know—grumble at the parsimony of European *restaurateurs* in the matter of that comestible. For myself the continually refilled miniature saucer of firm, fresh butter that is always beside my plate on the American table is a constant source of pleasure. And to all appearances it is supplied gratis, though whether it be or no I have no means of knowing since I have never looked at a bill in this country.

I don't look at bills—not because I am extravagant, or British, or plutocratic. In France or England I not infrequently examine a waiter's reckoning with some attention. In France you are not respected if you do not do it, and I do not care whether the English waiter respects me or not, so having learned the habit in Paris, I do not bother to discontinue it in London. But then in London and Paris I know the language. I don't mean to say that in New York or Chicago I should not understand the wounding things that a detected waiter might say to me—the point is that I should not know how to sass him back, whereas in either of the other metropolitan cities I enjoy making a scene in dishonest restaurants. I remember one ... That has nothing to do with American cooking but it has this American association for me in that we were taken for Americans—and South Americans at that—and treated as such. That is to say that we were—or rather my friend was—charged eighteen pounds odd or say ninety dollars for four indifferent dinners such as are served at monstrous and expensive caravansaries the world over, for three bottles of wine two of which were corked, and some liqueurs. With its sequelæ that made an agreeable evening.

But I do not mean to write of those large and despicable places which are all the same the world over. Their procedures are identical, find yourself in which hemisphere you may. They hire a famous chef. He has as a rule one special dish which he rides to death in the menu and only carefully prepares for the very rare customer who is well known to be captious. He has too many underlings to be able to superintend them properly and as a rule he lets them do as they will after a lesson or so. His hot plates—or whatever means he adopts of keeping dishes warm—keep dishes warm until they are tasteless, tepid, and entirely tedious. It is indeed the tediousness of meals in these places that is their chief characteristic even if the chef has distinguished himself over his special *plat*. For what is the good of eating canvas-back duck *à la* New Orleans, or *canard Rouennais*, or wild duckling with marrowfats and orange-peel sauce, be they never so delicious, if all the rest of the meal be tepid and slovenly? That is deep boredom. I would rather have a little bully beef, a raw onion, some good strong cheese, a leaf or so of cos lettuce and salt, some good crusty bread and plenty of fresh butter—and of course a bottle of hard old ale. I aver that I have had better appetite for such a meal—and better talk over it—than I have ever had for the most excruciatingly French-misnamed cookery in any of the Ritzes or Carltons or Splendides in any city of any continent. Of course their champagnes will stimulate the tongue, but personally I hate both champagne and the conversation it induces. Claret is the only wine over which to converse; *château neuf du pape* is good if you are tired and wish to soliloquize or talk heated politics; Burgundy is good to make love upon—but champagne is only good for the fag-end of dances, and in the form of cocktails for young ladies at that.

But what is this? . . . I am writing in Chicago. This is a daydream. I must have nodded. Here I drink ginger-ale with my meals, the water tasting nightmarishly of chlorine.

But how else is one to write of cooking? The purpose of meals is companionship, reminiscence and communion, otherwise they are mere stoking. And immensely much of the pleasure of consuming choice meats is geographical. How often when, at a really good board, you are dwelling on chicken with all its fixings will you not observe a dreamy look steal over the face of your dinner partner! Then you know that she is thinking of Maryland with its steamy fields at dusk when the chickens come to hand and the grasses are fragrant.

Or how often have we not dreamed of the Common and the Back Bay, or of Lexington, or Concord or the Adirondacks when we consumed *cassoulet de Castelnaudary,* which in its more commercial forms of the Paris restaurants is nothing but baked beans and pork? . . . Of course when you consume *cassoulet de Castelnaudary* in Castelnaudary I do not know what geographically you think about. You compose, I imagine, a *nunc dimittis.* I know I have done so. We had on that occasion between us two bottles of the most priceless 1906 Ch— But I know I must not. The *cassoulet* came off a fire that has never been extinguished since 1367 and that has always had a *cassoulet* on it. . . . And the sunlight beating down on the white road sent hot rays up through the jalousies and the commercial travelers cleaned their knives on the tablecloths and like the morning stars sang in their glory. Do you know what you sing on such occasions? It is

Aussitôt que la lumière vient entrer mes rideaux,
Je commence ma carrière par visiter mes tonneaux
Le plus grand roi . . .

But I *know* I must not.

The curious thing is that I cannot remember what I ate long, long ago in Baltimore or elsewhere in Maryland—except for watermelon which comes back to me as resembling a bath sponge that has sopped up some very weak sugared water. We used to cut chunks out of it with the machetes with which we cut the corn, and then we would return to cutting the corn beneath a vertical sun in the copper sky. I remember, too, sitting with my feet on a barrel at the store at crossroads, waiting with the rest of the inhabitants for the mail and consuming dried apple-rings from another barrel. And I used to wonder what could have been the cause of the subsequent nightmare. I remember, too, bringing numerous packages back from the store in the buckboard I was given to drive. I remember how the buckboard was tied together with bits of string and the harness with decayed rope. I still see the agile chestnut horses; I still feel the jolting over the roads which in England we should have called sand dunes and ravines because of the rocks; I remember the sun which in England we should have called a blast-furnace and the dust and the katydids. . . . But as for what was in those packages from which we presumably ate . . . nary bite!

But stay. There comes back to me succotash in little saucers which did not interest me. But corn grilled, or rather toasted on the cob! Ah, that I remember. I remember the butter dripping off the elbows in the kitchen of the colonial farmhouse where we ate. And, by a process of reasoning rather than by recollection of taste, I remember fried eggs and chicken on Sundays. I say process of reasoning because I remember the farmer saying that he dare not kill one of his own beasts or hogs because they were all marked down by the meat trust. You could not, he said, buy fresh meat between Baltimore or Philadelphia and San Francisco. Perhaps he was exaggerating.

At any rate I do not remember much of the rural food of Maryland or Pennsylvania in those days; but I do remember pleasurably certain foods in New England and New York. I never, I think, ate baked beans actually in Boston, but I do remember eating admirable beans in Fall River, Massachusetts, in a little frame-house, the property of a trolley conductor. He had begun by asking if I were English and then had said that his wife was English. I talked queer but not so queer as her. So he took me home to lunch with him. And there, sure enough, was his wife and, sure enough, she did talk queer for she was a Lancashire cotton-operative lassie speaking a dialect so broad that it was all I could do to understand her. So we cowered us down in i' th' ingle and had a gradely pow, while the beans were baking in the bean pot, which was as delicately browned as any meerschaum. She was a high-colored, buxom creature. I don't remember whether she had come to Fall River of her own accord to make her fortune in the cotton mills or whether the trolley conductor had visited Manchester and married her because she was a skilled cotton-operative. But she wore a shawl over her head for all the world as she might have done in Ancoats market, and in spite of it her beans were admirable —as good as the *cassoulet* of Parisian restaurants. I have certainly latterly never tasted anything so good. But that is perhaps prejudice.

You see, the other day, somewhere north of Boston, I read the wail of a New England gastronome. It was to the effect that, alas and alas, local comestibles no longer come from the designated localities. Boston beans come, the pork from Chicago, the beans from, say, Milwaukee; and they are all canned somewhere in the Middle West. And so with all food in America: it came, he said, out of tins—even canvas-back duck, Russian caviare, and soft-shelled crabs. That writer indeed averred that there were only two clubs in New York where you could be certain of eating genuine canvasback and you had to order it beforehand at that. He perhaps exaggerates!

How that may be I do not know. Standardization must have its victories that are more cruel than those of war. It is true that during the late War we had frequently to eat baked beans and mutton out of cans. I remember a first-class carriage on a siding outside Hazebrouck at one o'clock in the morning with the thermometer below zero and no windows in the carriage; and my bâtman heating one of those Mackonochie rations over three candles tied together; and our sharing it. And damned good it was. But to eat it in an apartment house in peace time, with no chance of even such exercise as running from shells would be pretty cruel.

Standardization and de-territorialization go on the world over. Last summer in Avignon in the south of France under the shadow of the Palace of the Popes, in a restaurant that I had found admirable for thirty years—I had, indeed, years ago eaten there in the company of Frederic Mistral, the Provençal poet—there, in that sacred and august shadow I was offered Norwegian anchovies with the *hors d'œuvres* and *pêche Melba* made with California peaches out of a tin. The Mediterranean that swarms with real anchovies was only fifty miles away, and Norway is seven hundred or so— and Heaven alone knows how far it is from California to Avignon, whilst in the spring whole hillsides of Provence are nacreous-pink with peach blossoms. But the peaches go to London; and Norwegians and Californians go to Avignon to eat their home products, and I come to New York to eat Mediterranean anchovies. It is perhaps not a mad world, but it seems a pretty queer one sometimes.

The gentlemen who write to the newspapers about the deterioration of their national cookings may perhaps be regarded with suspicion. They are apt to cry *O tempora! O mores!* because it is agreeable so to cry and, being usually oldish, their palates have frequently deteriorated. I daresay my own may have. And I usually avoid newspaper comments on food. I never can understand what sort of person writes them. Nevertheless, they are sometimes amusing. I have lately been reading a controversy between a writer in an anti-American English paper and another in a pro-German and, therefore, anti-English review published in New York. Says the one, "It is impossible to find anything decent to eat in New York"; and the other, "It is impossible to eat any London food." Cries the Briton, What price the shoulder of mutton at A's; the beefsteak, oyster and kidney pudding at B's; the quince and apple tart at C's; the beef *à la mode* at D's; the Welsh rarebit at E's; the entrées at F's; the dessert at G's? . . . all in London. Retorts the American, What about the *Sauerkraut* at H's, the *Kaiserschmorren* at I's; the *Limburger mit Pumpernickel* at L's; the *gedaempfte Gaenserbrust* at M's? . . . all in New York. And so the contest rages. Let us try to ascend into regions more serene.

Think of oysters. . . . There are few things that I have so frequently discussed with Middle-Westerners on the boulevards not of Chicago, Ill., but of Paris, France.

There are few things over which excited patriotisms are more hideously stirred. You may more safely blaspheme against the Tricolor, the Union Jack, or Old Glory than breathe a word against the blue point, the Whitstable native, or the Marenne. And on the boulevards where the battle of the

THE LORDLY DISH

oyster is daily waged during all the months that have r's in them I am frequently alarmed for fear knives should finish up these contentions.

The Americans allege that blue points alone are divinities amongst bivalves; they allege that all European oysters taste strongly of copper. The Europeans have naturally never tasted American oysters, but the idea that anything can be said against their sacred and nacreous sea-food with the traditions that go back to Caligula—*that* sets them foaming at the mouth. The subject last year so intrigued me that I one day determined to give the matter an exhaustive test. The idea occurred to me in Paris, in mid-September, and from that day to this I have consumed oysters daily and at almost every meal. In New England I have even had them for breakfast. This you will not believe, but I have. And well, I have eaten them in Paris, in New York, in Boston; and—though I was warned against it—in Chicago. I even wished to eat them in St. Louis, but I was there taken firmly in hand and given some sort of soup instead. I hate soup.

So imagining myself fairly qualified and being sure of my impartiality, I venture to give this verdict. It is incorrect to say that the European oyster tastes of copper. Indeed, how can the American gastronome know how copper tastes, whereas have not every Briton and every French child sucked coppers in his cradle? He ought not to do it but he does, so that few savors can be more familiar to him than that of the humble ha'penny. At any rate, it is familiar to me and I solemnly aver that what the European oyster tastes of is the sea—and that is why we love it. Whilst we devour it we see frigate-warfare in which the victories are won by Nelson or Villeneuve, according as we were born on one side of the blanket or the other; we see the limitless verges of eternal ocean; the blue of Capriote grottoes gleams translucently before our reminiscent eyes. And, as I have already said, one of the chief values of food is the reminiscential romance that it causes to arise.

The clam does taste of copper and, except in the form of clambake eaten on an open beach, I personally dislike it very much. But the blue point and the other American oysters are different. They are completely flavorless and they rely for their attraction on texture. For their flavor they have to fall back on such adjuncts as tomato catsup, horseradish sauce, and other excitants of the palate. They are, in short, different. No doubt if you have seen them in their beds or if you have consumed them on the shores of Nantucket they will make you see the ocean by means of their texture; but for me the only thing that happens when I eat a blue point is that I see the face of the nice person with whom I was eating when I first placed one of those morsels, duly dripping with cocktail sauce, between my lips. . . . That is good enough; *je ne demande pas mieux*. And by a curious coincidence, it was the same person who refused to allow me to eat oysters in St. Louis.

The singular flavorlessness of the American oyster impressed me so much that at first in my haste I averred that you might just as well take one of the little round crackers, butter it well, and soak it in cocktail sauce. But that is not true. I remember, by the bye, twenty-one years ago at Mouquin's—alas, there is no longer any Mouquin's—asking Miss Cather, whose name I permit myself the pleasure of mentioning, why she took horseradish sauce with her oysters. She replied, "Well, you see they have sometimes rather a funny flavor." But that was twenty-one years ago, and refrigeration has abolished that characteristic. Still it is not true that buttered cracker will really replace the blue point. I eat them frequently just for the flavor of the cocktail sauce but I don't then see any pleasant visions.

No, the real merit of the blue point as of the Cape Cod and their even vaster compatriots is their texture. If you could give the denizens of East Atlantic shallows that texture or if you could give their American relatives the European flavor then indeed you would have called the New World in to redress the balance of the Old. You can indeed convey their jolly plumpness to the Whitstable native and doubtless to the Marenne. I once kept a number of English deep-sea oysters in a shallow tub of frequently renewed sea-water, feeding them on very fine oatmeal the while, for about a fortnight. At the end of that time they were as plump as butter. . . . But they had completely lost all flavor! And they had not the pleasant—let me call it resilience—of the Westerner.

And of course, with its great varieties of size, the American oyster can give points and a beating in the matter of emotion. Its gamut is extraordinary. The Marenne or the Whitstable native—or even the humble Portuguese oyster, which resembles a teaspoonful of sea-water to which has been added a little gummy mud—all these you must eat in a sort of reverie so that your tongue may miss none of the passages of flavor. They should, I think, really be eaten in solitude. But over the American oyster you can converse freely, you can be gay, I daresay the young could even make love, as they can over Burgundy. Madame la Duchesse de Clermont-Tonnere in her admirable book on *les bonnes choses de la France* states that the favorite—the almost sole—comestible consumed in the *cabinets particuliers* of that pleasant land is the crayfish, the drink being Pommard, so that it is on the scarlet shells of those crustaceans rather than upon the nacreous blue-gray ones that you tread when mounting the stairs. How that may be I do not know but the duchess' assertion goes to prove my contention that the European oyster is an attendant upon reverie.

But it seems to me that you can do anything over any American sea food. I daresay you could even cry over a Cotuit, and as for me, when called upon to consume one of those things as large as soup plates that now and then come in one's way, I feel myself to be a cave-dweller, a real he-man, devouring young babies, having in each hand a half-gnawed shinbone with which I bash on the head my fellow guests to right and left.

I am now going to make a terrible confession: I find American food in practically *all* public places to be huge in size, splendid in appearance, but almost invariably as nearly flavorless as possible. That is not really an indictment of American cookery, but merely of the material employed and, if it is an indictment at all, it is meant to attach only to meals served in public places. For I want to make as strong a point as I can of the following statement, since it is the Great Truth about cooking. If I could I would print the whole in capitals so as the more firmly to rivet it on your attention. I am amazed when I hear Americans complain with heat and even as if with hatred that you cannot get decent food in England. These individuals I always ask at once, "Do you know any English families? Have you ever eaten in an English upper or upper middle-class home? Or have you ever even eaten in a first-class English club?" Of course they never have. You could exactly reverse the questions and the answers. And that is the Great Truth.

In wealthy—and still more in wealthyish—American homes the cooking is as admirable as it could be anywhere. I remember an American dinner which was cooked in Paris by a French woman whom the American family in question had taken with them to spend two years in this country. She had been an authentic *cordon bleu* to start with and she had picked up her American cooking from negresses in, I think, Kentucky. At any rate it was in the South. And this combination resulting in this particular dinner was as good as anything I have ever eaten. It was as good as anything could possibly be. That was American cooking.

But if you reproduced the same sort of circumstances for English cooking—I mean that if you took a French cook and installed her for two years in England in such circumstances as would let her assimilate the knowledge of English "good plain" or "professed" cooks, the dishes she would cook on returning to Paris would be just as admirable. They might, indeed, be better. Except for the wine—since you cannot get good wine in England!—they might really be better if she remained in London where materials are better than they are in Paris—at any rate in the department of meat and fish.

That would be English cooking. For there is no sense in talking of any national cooking except in terms of meals produced by really skilled professional practitioners in moderately wealthy homes, the meals to be composed of first-rate materials. For it is to be remembered that cooking begins before the kitchen is reached, the selection of foods being almost as important as their preparation or their heating and dishing up. I cannot, of course, claim to have any very intimate knowledge of the materials that are at the disposal of the American professed family cook. I have taken the trouble to visit one or two markets and to examine the meats, fish, and fruits displayed. They all seem to me to suffer from standardization, and certainly they all do seem to suffer from cold storage or refrigeration. But that very good material can be obtained in this country I know because of innumerable meals that I have eaten in kindly and hospitable families.

American public meals are horrible—but so are English public meals and so, for the matter of that, are French, German, Italian, and Spanish Anglo-Saxonized ones. For, in the matter at least of cookery, the world suffers from overcommunication and too efficient transport. I dare say that in California even Californian apples, oranges, or figs may have some flavor. They certainly have not in London, New York, Boston, Avignon, or Strasbourg. That may, of course, be due to transport, but I happen to have paid some slight—of course mainly epistolary—attention to the matter of fig-culture in the Far West, and I believe it to be due in that case to climate and soil—the most delicious of small Italian brown figs becoming almost as entirely tasteless and fibrous as the native Californian fruit within a year or so after transplantation. But it is not merely the transporting of food materials from one end of the world to the other that is responsible for the dead monotony, inedibility, and indigestibleness of all western European and farther Occidental public cooking. I sometimes think that, long before the invention of wireless telegraphy, *restaurateurs* and restaurant cooks must have developed some thirteenth or fourteenth sense by which from the Prado to the Lido and from the Strand to the banks of the Nile and back again to the shores of Lake Michigan they have telepathically communicated their terrible secrets of the preparation of tepid underdone beef, sauces compounded in imitation of billstickers' paste, *côte de veaux Clamart,* chicken cutlets, and the even more unnameable vegetable horrors that you are called upon to eat amongst marble and gilding, with spiky palm leaves threatening to tickle the back of your neck, to the sound of standardized jazz or standardized Tzigane or Viennese waltzes. As far as I am concerned, the best public meals I have eaten I ate lately in Chicago.

These things run in strata. Below these gilded atrocities are to be found the Cimmerian box-shaped caves where eat the poorer white-collared classes—the clerks and stenographers who are the ball-bearings of our civilization. Here you may reach the lowest depths of despondency over imitation-marble table tops. I say despondency because whether in London, in New York, in Birmingham, Manchester, or any other American or British provincial city to eat regularly in these places you must not only feed without interest but you must have arrived at a state of being without hope, and so your digestion will color your mentality with the gloomier shades of despair.

The curve goes upward in the strata socially below this. I have eaten in what we call "good pull-ups for carmen," cabmen's shelters, and the like in I don't know how many European cities, and in several American ones, and I have never in one of them come across food that was not admirable in quality, if usually a thought tough, roughly served, of course, but always piping hot and well-flavored. That is because that class of human beings—the men who drive horses in wagons, or motor lorries, who haul heavy burdens about the world and up to sixth or fourteenth floors—goes to make up the one Occidental city class which takes a keen interest in its food. It needs good keenly flavored viands to crush between its powerful teeth and it sees that it gets them. Its subsequent labors take care of its digestion.

It sees that it gets them. . . . The whole moral of the world of food considered as a delight lies in those words. Except by accident or when making purposed excursions for the purpose of this writing, I have lived as well, I have found as good food and as well cooked, in New York as I habitually do in Paris. That is because if I may express a he-man's sentiments in soldierly language I damn well see that I get it. It takes some trouble, it means exploring nooks and corners, mostly in the basements of obscure streets. But it can be done. It might be done by everybody.

It might be done and Anglo-Saxondom should do it, as they used to say of the Northwest Passage. I have spent some time lately in examining with attention the weekly menus afforded presumably for nonwealthy households by the cookery experts of Sunday papers of many cities in this continent, and all I can say is that when reading them I have felt precisely the same profound dejection which has been mine when perusing similar diet sheets in Great Britain. And I know something about it. For a long period of time I prepared the weekly diet sheets for large units of His Britannic Majesty's expeditionary force. Nay, I even waged an eternal war in the course of which I was frequently disciplinarily but not morally bruised—a war with the Command in Chief of the culinary branch of the service. In private life the gentleman who commanded this arm of our forces was the director of one of those immense concerns that spread indigestion, ennui, and despondency through sixty per cent of the thirteen million population of the capital of our empire. He would produce for my guidance diet sheets that might have been compiled by Isabel of the *New York Sunday Eagle* or Dora of the *Liverpool Weekly Herald*. There was the same superfluity of what I believe is called in this country "roughage" and the same complete want of anything with any taste to it. I for my part completely ignored his orders; I gave my men as many savory, small portions as the food at my disposal

THE LORDLY DISH

and the industry of my cooks could command. I tried to contrive that frying was done with animal and, if possible, with pork fat; I nibbled coppers away from money allotted to the awful things called in this country cereals and spent it on condiments. In France I even bartered small quantities of, say, hominy-ration for garlic. All hell broke loose over my battalions; The G. O. C. i. C. Messing launched worse than papal bulls at my head. But my men were contented, alert, cheerful, good at drills, admirable marksmen, and perfect demons with the bayonet. . . . And I was not shot.

The dreadful topic of "roughage" needs a whole volume to itself. I must limit myself here to the briefest moral summing up. Happiness, contentment, alertness, clear eyes, bright crisp hair—and even, who knows? consummate salesmanship!—can come only from eating many small portions of food that you really like and that is so savory that your mouth waters in anticipation. It is by the water of your mouth that your eyes will be made to shine. You must eat, when you eat in restaurants, in tiny places—they can be found in New York—where there are no gilding, palms, or music. The money that might have been spent on those will there be put into the viands and the wages of the cook. You must talk frequently to the proprietor about his menus and discuss what you eat with your wife or your fellow guest. And above all you must eat what you like and only what you like. You must also see that garlic is in your food but only in sufficient quantities to accentuate the flavor, not to have a taste of its own. You will object that in that case you will be distinguished by an unpleasing odor. But in a whole gay population which consumes garlic you yourself, having consumed it and being gay, will not be so distinguished, neither will your neighbors.

Those terrible inquisitors, the physicians of to-day, have discovered that in garlic is to be found the real fountain of youth. So they are prescribing it for you—for almost all complaints—but synthetically and flavorlessly. The doctor is like the priest. He tries to kill joy, but along the lines of your superstitions and fears. We—you and I Anglo-Saxons—are trying to-day with our cookery to condone the sins of our Puritan ancestors. It is the only Puritanism that remains in New York, which is not America, and also in Great Britain, which is not yet America. So we let the physician replace the priest to whom we no longer resort; and the doctor, knowing that our

THE LORDLY DISH 213

superstitions trend that way, knowing that we think it sinful to take a delight in the palates that the good God has given us for our health and delight—the doctor insists that we eat things tasteless, uncondimented, unassoiled, unblest—and horribly productive of what in this country is, I believe, called "gas," but to which our grosser shepherds give a more romantic name.

Let us, then, limit the term the American cuisine, to the admirable, the almost perfect, meals that negroes here prepare in their culinary ecstasies. For no negress knows how she cooks. Neither do I when I cook. I use everything within sight in a frenzy resembling a whirlwind, and it takes an army of scullery maids to clean up the kitchen after me. But you won't have a headache after a hogshead of their—or my—cooking.

Let me finish with a story—for people like stories. When I was last in London I listened to a dialogue of two young women of the shop-assistant type on the top of a bus. Says the first, "You aren't out with your toff to-night?" Says the second, "No, I says to 'im, 'Charley, you've 'ad me out every night this week. We've bin to Lyon's Corner House, to the A. B. C., to the Carlton Grill, and the Savoy. I don't know where we 'aven't bin. And what I says is,

"Give me a rest. Let me stop at 'ome and eat something out of a tin." ' "

I thought it might have been New York. And upon my soul I don't know whether I ought to have rejoiced because the populace is revolting against the food provided in public places or whether I ought to have cried *O tempora! O mores!*

CHAPTER VII

REGIONS CÆSAR NEVER KNEW. . . .

SO that I am forced back upon the position from which I set out . . . that allowing for changes in circumstances humanity is much the same the world over. American cookery is much the same . . . is very little better and very little worse than cookery the world over. Americans, that is to say, who pay attention to cookery get better cooking than people in other countries who do not. The reverse is also true. . . . On the whole I should be inclined to give a little prize to the Westerners because of the little, unexplainable dish of butter with which I began my last chapter. For me that has sanctified many indifferent meals; but as I say I cannot explain it. Is butter singularly cheap in the United States . . . or is there a clause about it in the Declaration of Independence? I should imagine not; but there is no knowing. I have never met any one in the United States who has ever read that document. . . . For the matter of that I found myself at table the other day with half a dozen well-educated Americans and of that company I was the only one who knew the name of the first settlement founded by the pilgrim fathers. . . . I was caused to turn my attention to these historico-international matters rather more than ten years ago, before the late war, by an American—a New England—lady who assurred me with singular and impressive animus that the mince-pie was unknown in England. She was not saying that English mince-pies were not so good as New England mince-pies. . . . And indeed I may insert here the statement that the best mince-pie I have ever tasted I ate lately in Park Avenue, here, at the house of a Philadelphia lady who has spent most of her life in England and France. And the pie was cooked by an inhabitant of the country of France where mince-pie is unknown except as a very rare Xmas import from London. . . . But that long ago New England lady stated with tears—almost—in her voice that I hated America. And because I hated America I wanted to deprive New England of the credit of having invented the mince-pie. . . .

Well, I can only say that there is a statute of Oliver Protector forbidding the English to eat mince-pie on Sundays—so mince-pie must have been known in England in the days of the Commonwealth. Of course one of the Pilgrim Fathers—for I believe the Pilgrim Fathers set out for Plymouth before the days of Cromwell—one of them may have sent back a letter by the returning Mayflower describing how he baked plum-frumity in shallow pie-crust. Because there exist quite a number of Elizabethan receipts for making plum-frumity and if you made dishes according to those receipts you would have to-day what we call mince-meat. And it is no good saying that Raleigh brought back that receipt from New England because Raleigh never went to New England—and there exists a fourteenth-century English receipt for making a Conceit or Device in which what to-day we call mince-meat is recommended to be baked in pie-crust. It is true that the pie-crust ought to be shaped in the form of a square castle and gilded. But there was the mince-pie—and as far as I can remember Columbus had not committed his indiscretion before 1332. . . . And what English person does not know that for every mince-pie you eat in a different house between Xmas and Twelfth Night you will have a happy month in the ensuing year? . . . How many mince-pies have I not eaten under the compulsion of that belief . . . and how many doctors have not profited by it? But, curiously enough, only yesterday morning or so whilst in a breakfast-car just west of Altoona I was accused by a lady from Boston who sat casually opposite me of hating America—because I do not like salad. So history repeats itself. That quite charming, rather fresh, gray-haired, true Puritan descendant from Plymouth days said to me: "I guess you are English and hate America or you would not say that about American salads." . . . For I will confess that I have suffered, oh, *dreadfully!* from the American habit of introducing salads at any, at the most unexpected, points of their meals. I hate salads; I do not believe that any one should eat any raw green vegetables unless he is certain exactly where and how it was grown and then only if he has seen it cut and washed. I would certainly never eat salad either in Paris or China. . . . Still, that is only a personal obsession. I am not saying that salads should not be eaten by other people; that it is bad taste to eat salad, or anything like that. I mean that I am not condemnatory. Only that I have suffered. (There are people who do not like butter.)

Still, the case of those last is not so bad.

REGIONS CÆSAR NEVER KNEW ... 219

You can leave your butter saucer beside your plate untouched and no one will notice. Salad is different. Of course if you eat in a public restaurant you can refrain as long as you are careful to see that your guests do not go without. But it is my happy fate to receive a quite extraordinary amount of hospitality in this country . . . and then my trouble begins. Being a foreigner and guest I am generally seated beside the hostess . . . and the hostess is almost invariably proud of her salad. . . . I will tell you. . . . I was seated the other day at the hospitable board that I most like to attend in all the city of New York—beside the New York hostess that I most like. 'Well, the room was beautiful and the hostess, and the appointments and the guests; the food was as good as I have ever eaten, the wines—yes, the wines! —unexceptionable, from a pre-war cellar. And then. . . . After the most delectable small birds and fixings that you can imagine there was served a salad. . . . Of alligator pears and shrimps!

Now alligator pears are the most delicious things in the world . . . *naturel,* and eaten if possible in the open air. But here they were sliced with a dreadful—oh, a *dreadful*—dressing of a purplish color. And shrimps are all very well in their way, in sauce with fish, or out of sauce if they are large enough and some one else is at the pains of peeling them for you. But here they were with a sort of Thousand Island dressing. And alligator pears! You know . . . it was too much. I looked at my hostess and said, after I had tasted that salad:

"I can't. . . . Oh I *can't!*"

The most intense concern came over her face as she said:

"Oh, I am so sorry. I invented that salad for you, myself" And there it stood on the menu . . . *Salade à la Ford!*

Now I do not know if I look or talk like a man who would like alligator pears with shrimps and Thousand Island dressing. I suppose I do, and the thought is bitter. But still more bitter is the fear that I may not be asked to that house again. Better men have been cut off less cherished visiting lists for smaller offenses. . . . And I believe that hostess to be *exigeante*. She told me indeed during that meal that she had, precisely, cut off her visiting list during the first two years of Prohibition every man who came drunk to her house or had there exceeded. . . . So I may not be asked again: after all one's sobriety may well be doubted if one refuses alligator pears. . . . A bitter thought. Still that was only two days ago; I may yet.[1] And one eats even worse salads. I have had to. I invented myself, years ago, a salad of celery, apples and walnuts. I gave it up after trial. Here it meets me every day. . . . But most detestable of all is a sweet macedoine of fruits with oil and vinegar dressing. The people who give you that are the sort of people who never have olive oil—and the best cottonseed oils and other substitutes have nauseating, sweetish afterflavors.

Now as regards the lady in the Gotham express—I was on the way, here, to Chicago—I had, just to make conversation and a little for instruction, for I seldom get opportunities of conversing with Bostoners—they not liking my ribald habit of mind—I had asked her then why she ate salad; whether she liked it or whether she regarded it as a duty.

She flushed, suspecting that I was poking fun at the New England Conscience. Mind, I had said nothing against salads. But immediately she had jumped to the conclusion that I was English and hated America. And that, indeed, is how most international misunderstandings are caused to arise. For, at any rate at that moment I was feeling

[1] Note later. I have.

quite remarkably a New Yorker, having been as it were violently thrown back upon Gothamism by the contemplation of the terrible, brown-snow-covered flats of the Middle West. . . . She, on the other hand, was traveling to somewhere in the neighborhood of, let us say, Terre Haute, Indiana, where she proposed to recover from a nervous breakdown caused by overwork of a sedentary and responsible kind on Beacon Hill. . . . It seemed to be a curious place to which to go amidst the snow for the purpose of curing sick nerves. But I think there were relatives farming there who had come from the neighborhood of Williamstown, Mass.

She was, as I have said, gray-haired, very fresh colored, tall and extremely thin but charming with the charm that Mary E. Wilkins used to impart into her New England spinsters of a quarter of a century since. She ate for breakfast a poached egg, a salad of lettuce with French dressing and a measured quantity—I should imagine about three ounces—of some sort of maize-flour bread with a measured teaspoonful of butter. She drank imitation coffee without milk and with one lump of sugar. . . . She said that she was trying to gain weight. But having eaten that breakfast she sighed and said:

"Oh, I suppose I may as well get it over

now!" and she ordered another poached egg. Then she looked over at me and with troubled brows explained that her doctor ordered her to consume two eggs a day. She *hated* eggs. So it was a question of going through the day to find a meal at which her courage would let her consume those eggs. Sometimes she would eat one at breakfast and one at lunch. Sometimes she would shudder through two at lunch. Sometimes —horribly—she would find herself near bedtime with both uneaten. Then she would have them both, in a crisis of revulsion, beaten up with some milk.

I had remarked that a doctor who ordered his patient to consume food from which his stomach revolted, with the idea of fattening his patient, could not be much of a doctor. The essence of making food nourish and therefore fatten a patient lay in prescribing for him what he liked; otherwise the gastric juices did not function and the food was improperly digested. I said indeed incautiously that a really healthful meal was made up of food at the anticipation of which your mouth watered. She said that that was a horrible idea. She said that she would never *think* of telling her doctor what she liked or did not like: it was your duty to like what was good for the majority of humanity. It was your duty, too, never to think of what you liked or did not like. She was beginning, meanwhile, shudderingly, on her second egg.

It had been then that I had asked her if she really liked salad. I am, as you see, a little mad on that subject and I had gone a little madder since seeing the menu of a 35-cent lunch, lately, at a great department store. It consisted of two kinds of bread, one of maize-meal, the other of flour, a salad of endive with French dressing, or, alternatively, a fruit salad with the same sort of dressing, a cup of tea... and ice-water unlimited. And the thought of the mothers and wives of a great city that I loved martyrized in the midst of their hard days' labors for keeping the home together with nothing but those gaseous horrors to sustain them had indeed driven me a little madder than ever. ... But I had had no propagandist or interested motives in putting that question. I had just wanted to know whether that unknown lady really liked salad or ate it merely as a matter of duty. ...

And after she had unmasked my nationality and had asserted that I was still thirsting for revenge over Bunker's Hill, Boston, she continued, flushing more deeply and with quite exaggerated animus:

"Of course I like salad or I should not eat it. I eat it three times a day—at breakfast, lunch and dinner. I should eat it four times if I thought it right to eat four meals a day. Besides it contains the largest known quantity of Vitamin No. 3."

I continued, however, remorselessly:
"Did you always like salad? Or did you only develop a taste for these debauches of raw greenstuff after you had heard about the Vitamins?"

She began at once spiritedly. Of course she had always liked salads. She had always eaten. . . . But then she hesitated. Her love for truth was too great; much as she would have desired to add another victory to Bunker's Hill by confounding me, she said: No, she could not remember. She had never much considered her food. But she imagined that she had certainly eaten more salads since she had heard of Vitamins.

So I let it go at that, though I had wanted to tell her that the consuming of food that you liked was good for you because it was an instinct implanted in you by protective nature, whereas to acquire with effort a taste for eating food that you disliked was as bad as acquiring any other unnatural appetite. But I was on no propagandist mission; I should only have pained her and should have done her no more good than I shall do to my present, unknown reader. A magic word like Vitamin 3 will send a whole race, a whole humanity, plunging to destruction like the Gadarene swine. And who am I to interrupt that catastrophe? ... So I will let that alone along with the consideration of all the train of inhibitions and complexes, nation- and world-wide that are involved with it. .... I only told that lady that my personal rule of life was to do what I wanted and take what I got for it. She remarked cheerfully:

"How very English! Do the English still think like that?"

I said: "Heaven forbid! The English think extraordinarily as you do."

But she ignored me, continuing that it was strange that we should be so unchanged considering all the lessons we must have had and adding that she had often deplored our terrible conditions and even sometimes thought we deserved some respect for the brave fight we were making against hopeless odds. But what would you have? . . .

I gathered in fact that she considered that I and all my compatriots were starving because we did not model ourselves on Beacon Hill. . . . And that will always seem a queer point of view to us because we have always considered that Boston was what it was because Beacon Hill modeled itself on the more intellectual parts of the suburb of Hampstead, London, Eng. That, however, is as near having an international conversation as I have in late years come on the Western side of the Atlantic. I feel myself here so unobservantly at home that, although I am not above having a little fun at the expense of any local patriotism anywhere, I should feel much more inclined to do it with some malice at the expense of an inhabitant of Manchester, Eng., a city which I detest, than at that of any Chicagoan, or citizen of Indianapolis or any settler near, let us say again, Terre Haute, Ind. That is perhaps because I don't know Chicago or Indianapolis or Terre Haute and I did once know Manchester. . . . But certainly I have felt less strange in those places than in say Birmingham, Leeds and Middlesboro'. . . . Boston is another matter, for it has always seemed to me to be difficult to believe that the Hub can be greater than the Whole.

The train, however, slid along over the unending plains, the pallid reflections from the brown snow usually gliding over our faces up to the ceiling of the car. . . . But every now and then that light would be cut off by horrors in the way of mine-shafts and other black things. And, not being in the mood to continue on discussions I began to reflect on the nature of plains.

I like plains—in the sense that I intensely dislike having to climb anything at all and that I am fond of riding a bicycle in level country. . . . But here the plains seemed to commit what I will call the sin of enormity and I was conscious of a slightly stifling feeling—a feeling of stifling added to that inseparable from riding in Pullman coaches. . . . I was hundreds of miles from the sea.

I had felt the same in Middle Europe, but here I had superadded a sensation of mournfulness that in Middle Europe and even in New England I should never feel. . . . There were no old buildings. I don't mean to say that there was nothing dilapidated. The farms near enough to see were mostly singularly unpainted, gardenless and in the mournful light endlessly depressing under the drab, low-running snow-clouds. . . . I don't mean to say that even a New England landscape, say up towards the foothills of the White Mountains, cannot be mournful enough with its deserted farms, its dilapidated fences, its ruined orchards under the snow. But at least, with its rolling hills, its small ravines, there is an end to it for the eye as there is an end to it as a civilization. Here there is none; to the landscape there is no end and the farming in the sad farms or the industrial occupations in the sad industrial towns may well go on for ever and ever. . . . Mind, I am not writing this as one who knows; I will write as one who knows a good deal more in a minute. Here I am merely describing my own feelings at entering—at finding with a sudden catch of the breath that I had awakened *in*— AMERICA.

For New England—farming New England whether with or without Boston as make-weight, is not America; what of it remains old New England is only Old England hardened in type. Even New England cooking is only English country cooking—hardened in type. You will get just the same in English cottages and farms—the chicken pot pie just the same, the boiled dinner exactly the same as our boiled silverside with vegetable additions, the baked beans just the same as our haricot mutton, and the pies just the same but a little less heavy in the crust—and the censoriousness, and the scandals, and the dreadful tales of unimaginative cruelties. A little harder perhaps in New Hampshire than in the old one. But not much. . . .

Still that life is very much passing. I saw from the train the other day an unroofed farm that I remember years and years ago, near Canaan, and then it contained its stalwart owner whose family had owned it since it was a settlement. . . . But he was married to the Italian maid of some summer boarders at a nearby summer resort and so dreadfully poor that he could not afford even a newspaper, let alone decent clothes. . . . Well, it was obvious even then that he would not much longer stick on there. Now it is equally obvious that he has gone. . . . There is some dairy farming in the bottoms; dagoes do some truck farming near the cities . . . which means in English that Italians raise cabbages and lettuce. Here and there in foothills—I believe more in the State of New York than elsewhere—a sort of dreadfully hard, superstitious, peasant population still clings harshly to the rocks, much as they still do in parts of the South. But that is not America. There was no doubt a time when agricultural New England could typify the New World. But it cannot any longer. Life there is too hard, too uneasy, too much of a struggle.

And there does there linger, in spite of the dagoes truckfarming and the alien dairymen, a sense of oldness . . . of old frames of mind. You can look out of the train at a little dale, covered with snow as if over a lawn, broken by a little stream, with a shack of sorts overhung by bare apple-trees. You can imagine yourself getting down at the little frame-house of the station where will be your sledge with the blanketed, fine, free-moving local-bred horse. The familiar expressman with his silver-rimmed spectacles will greet you with parcels. The sledge piled high, you will drive, buried in peltry, over the smooth snow to the shack where some one you like very much awaits you. And there would be the great fire and the brown eyes and the soft voice and the long night beneath the snow . . . the sound of the horse munching his oats in the warm stable that, I hasten to add, your fairy tale must have provided, coming to you through the board-walls of the shack.

But here in the plains I do not believe that day dream would visit you. You would have to drive miles and miles along wet, swamped tracks, on brick roads if you were lucky, with the water swishing over the axles . . . of your Ford. And you would leave the poor thing out of doors, under the snow.

Yet here again I must utter my warning that I am not setting down what is my own private preference as if it should be regarded as an infallible standard of taste. There is no reason why you should regard the quiet day dream amongst oldish things as the only occupation for a proper man any more than there is any reason why you should not regard a Ford car left out in the snow as being as proper an ending for a fairy tale as a horse munching beans in a warm stable. The one would be nearly as modern as the other to Julius Cæsar, who, if he drove anything, drove a quadriga that could not turn round; yet he was no doubt at least as exclusive in his tastes and modern in his point of view as you or I. And these are the regions Cæsar never knew, swayed in the end by the posterity of Boadicea.

And, again, I am painfully aware that some one may come along and assert that even the unending plains through which the trains proceed with the air of being out upon eternal, level journeys—even those plains are not America. Some one is always ready to say to me, even in the Middle West itself: "Ah, this is not AMERICA. You do not know America until you have seen the Coast." And gentlemen from the South tell me that the West is not America, and young women from Seattle tell me that New Mexico is not *America*.

So that the one thing I am certain of is what I set out with . . . that New York is not America . . . and of that I am certain—certain sure—because all, all the rest, the inhabitants of Terre Haute, of Seattle, of Los Angeles, of St. Augustine, of Norfolk, Va., or Boston, Mass. . . . all, all the rest of the inhabitants of the Republic of the United States of North America will assure you that New York is not that. . . . But who then has seen America? I don't know. Surely no American. I know one person who has been in thirty-eight states of the Union. He was born in Hoboken and lives in Paris. I know another—a born New Yorker—who has been in all the forty-eight states. The only person I have ever met who has, she was taken the round of the states on successive trips organized by her (New York) school because it was considered to be the duty of a New Yorker to know his or her country. And she spends the greater part of her time in Europe and is certainly more familiar with the *mises à mort* of Seville, Spain, than with the stockyards of Chicago which, Middle Westerners assure me, are the true heart of America. . . . Well, I have never seen them and do not propose to.

So I am going to take the bit between my

teeth, amid most of all this confusion, and boldly to assume that the Middle West *is* America. . . . As such it is productive of disillusionment to the casual visitor.

I have spent my life—I seem to have spent my life—amongst Middle Westerners. I have, that is to say, passed periods in England, in France, in Belgium, in Germany, in Wales—and in New York. But set beside the Middle Westerners the relatively quiet inhabitants of these other places hardly seem to bulk on the map. The late War itself was a quiet affair compared with some gatherings of Middle Westerners in Europe that it has been my good fortune to attend. So, very naturally one figured them as born on the backs of mustangs with bowie knives in their teeth and leading subsequently lives compared to which the lives of Brett Harte's mining camp gamblers were parlor games.

But alas . . . the most truculent of these heroes was born in Oak Park. Oak Park is a suburb of Chicago—a very pleasant place with a number of trees on its boulevards and seats set up, as the inscriptions tell you, by members of the Oak Park Rotary Club. I have been to Oak Park. . . . Well, I myself was born in Merton, Surrey, then in the country but now a suburb of London. And I can assure you that Merton

Surrey is not one-half as decorous as Oak Park, Ill. And it is rather more dangerous. For it abuts on Wimbledon Common, where there are real ponds and on Sunday golfballs there fly about quite thickly. . . . And at Oak Park I interrogated a junior relation of my ferocious friend as to his ideals. He was a charming little boy of, say, twelve. He said that his ambition was eventually to drive the Flying American between Chicago and New York. . . . Well, at his age, in Merton, my ambition was to drive the Flying Dutchman—still the fastest train in the world—360 miles in 359 minutes non-stop. Something like that. . . . But, of course, one does not mention that in Oak Park.

So I gather that the occupations and ambitions of the suburbs are much the same whether in Chicago or London. There are many more Ford cars in Chicago but there are many more people in London; you have to allow for such differences!

And it was much the same with the homes of the other ferocious Middle Western friends of mine that I have been hospitably allowed to visit. These were mostly quite quiet farmsteads standing rather unsheltered in great fields. In very great fields where life is completely uneventful. But one completely uneventful life in one very great field is very much like another. My country cottage outside Paris stands on the edge of a very great field. It runs as far as the eye can reach almost level, a very little undulating. A few clumps of trees scatter themselves here and there, anywhere between your eye and the horizon. There are a few whitish gray farms, too, here and there —badly in need of painting. It goes on like that for miles and miles and miles.

It is in short the Middle West. The second most ferocious of my Middle Western friends coming to call on me, confronted suddenly with that prospect round the house-end, fell back a step or two and exclaimed:

"This is outside Lincoln, Nebraska!"

His particular form of truculence was to dilate on the immense, empty silences of the Middle West. At any moment on the Boulevards he would stop and exclaim: "Oh, but the great desolate silences . . ." Thus conveying an idea of himself as the essential, strong silent man—a sort of immense *Penseur* by Rodin dominating a thousand miles of empty land. . . . As a matter of fact he was born in a newspaper office of a rather large Middle Western town and the rest of his life had been spent in and around newspaper offices, mostly in the East.

On the other hand, Middle Westerners born and having lived all their lives on farms hundreds of miles from a city are fond of representing themselves as perfectly remorseless Chicago speculators, ruining millions by their Napoleonically unmoved operations in the Wheat Pit. And then there are people born in North Carolina who like to convey that they are natives of the Great Wild Plains, and natives of Indiana who like to convey that they are really refined Southern gentlemen. . . . I do not mean to say that they have not these feelings; not lying but romance moves them. . . . And there are immense stretches of territory where you find only Swedes and other immense stretches of territory where German is your only language. . . . One is told nevertheless that all these . . . *all* these, whilst retaining their native tongues, raiment, foods, habits and modes of thought become in some subtle way American and so meant by providence to rule New York, which is not American.

I was, that is to say, told by a quite serious, educated and unimpulsive gentleman that he lived—somewhere near Chesterton, Indiana, I think—in a community where he was the only adult born American, all the rest being either Danes or Mecklenburgers.

Nevertheless he quite seriously stated that these agriculturists had so assimilated the American spirit that they were better Americans than his own first cousins who had migrated from the state of Missouri, where they had been born, to New York. He stated that quite seriously, as I have said, and with equal seriousness and good humor added that if New York did not bend to the will of the American citizens of his township —in such matters as Prohibition and the religion of its governor—New York would have eventually to be controlled, if necessary, by force of arms.

I pointed out that in that case aliens, many of them not even naturalized, were better Americans than a great body of American-born citizens—that in fact Americanism, in his view, was a frame of mind rather than a question of territorialism or state allegiance. To this he quite agreed. I, I may state, was not arguing with him; I was merely trying to obtain information. And he emphasized and strengthened what I had advanced. Americanism, he said, was a point of view. . . . And he would go further. In his view good, honest, sober, industrious and Protestant farmers still in Denmark, or elsewhere in Scandinavia and North Germany were morally better Americans than a great proportion of the inhabitants at least of the Eastern States. Not politically of course—but every gain of a European nation for Prohibition was a world-gain for Americanism. ... I may add that this gentleman was an upper official in the United States Consular Service, so that he knew both the United States and North Europe.

I had come curiously enough across touches of the same frame of mind in the Boston lady of the two poached eggs. For, after she had finished the latter of those abhorred eatables, she invited me to accompany her to the look-out car at the end of the train so that I might observe something that I had never observed before. ... And in that invitation the slight, not in the least unpleasant, pleasure that she had in contemplating my British ignorance of so vast and vastly resourceful a country triumphed over the fact that she much disliked the aspect of the country and condemned its inhabitants for their lack of culture as compared with that of the dwellers on Beacon Hill. ... She told me incidentally that she felt very triumphant at having polished off her eggs because she would now have her mind free for the rest of the day. So she would be able to study with attention an immense body of literature in the form of press cuttings that she had got together, and alternately practice on the typewriter that was to be found in the parlor car—a complete mastery of that instrument not being as yet amongst her accomplishments.

In the observation car she pointed out to me the rails of the line running perfectly level in a perfectly diminishing perspective between the brownish snow to the lowering horizon and she asked me if I was not thrilled to think that those rails ran like that for a great many miles. . . . Seven thousand, I think she said. Or perhaps not so many.

I said that I was not thrilled—nor do I believe that she was—only she thought that foreigners ought so to be. I said that I disliked the thought and the sight very much. It emphasized one's sense of impotence; it was as bad as looking at the night sky and considering that the nearest star was seven thousand million miles away. I said I liked plains to have a border of hills; I said that once you stood in a plain with a completely unbroken horizon all round you it made no difference to you at that moment whether the plain continued for seven thousand miles or only for seventy and that if you moved into another, adjacent complete horizon it made no difference to you then, either. So, it made no difference. She said it did make a difference because of the hurricanes that swept unbroken across its surface and I said that that did not make me like it any better. She said that I ought to like to contemplate places where the wonders of nature occurred and I said that if they were not actually taking place the thought of them could be just as impressive on Fifth Avenue, whilst if they were going to take place I should prefer not to be there.

It is in that way that internatioal discussions are carried on. . . . But when we had finished talking through our hats she patted her great leather wallet of newspaper cuttings with an almost girlish satisfaction and said that she was now going to gather ammunition. She was usually employed in organization work for some religious association—I did not catch what. The work being very hard and she having no domestic help for herself and her aged father she had had a nervous breakdown, so that her brain had not hitherto allowed her to follow the matter of the cuttings. They concerned themselves with Prohibition—being either arguments in favor of that measure by distinguished Prohibitionists, statistics going to show the harm resulting from the use of alcohol, or accounts of individual calamity caused by that use. . . . And she said with the same almost girlish pleasure and with the triumph that had attended her swallowing of her last egg:

"Now I shall be able really to post myself on the subjects that are nearest my heart."

Now odd as it may appear that was the first time I had ever met a Prohibitionist. Of the hundreds and hundreds of Americans I have met—and I suppose I have met by now at least as many Americans as the average private American citizen meets in the course of his life—that was the first American I had ever met who was a Prohibitionist, at any rate to let me know it. And most Americans one has met during the last four years have indicated decisively enough, either by their tongues or their conditions, in which way their convictions lay. I do not mean to say that I believe the American in the majority to be wet; there is no means of knowing how the majority may to-day be. But I am at least aware that there are many, many millions of American Prohibitionists.

And I may as well add that I hold no views on the subject—or rather no one preponderating view. If it were ever my fate—which I pray that it may not be—to have to vote either for or against Prohibition in my own country I should be sore put to it by my conscience. I have on the one hand the strongest possible repulsion from interfering compulsorily with the morals of my fellow beings. I do indeed regard that as the greatest sin that one human being can commit against another and I am lost in amazement that any human being can be found with the courage to undertake the task. On the other hand, I do believe that the evils caused by drink are so terrible, so profound and so far-reaching that if a law could be framed that would effectively—absolutely effectively!—render all consumption of alcoholic liquor impossible I should be horribly hard put not to vote for it. I may add that before Prohibition had exercised the influence that it has on the habits of Americans that I know and still more on those that I have seen in public places in Europe and here, I held no very strong views against drink—or even against drunkenness. But till then I had never witnessed its effects on any great scale, nor, as far as I can remember, had I experienced them. I wish I could say the same to-day, after a comparatively short visit to this country.

And I have no hesitation in saying that much—that most—of the American drunkenness that I have seen has been the direct effect of Prohibition; I know too many Americans who before the passing of the Volstead Act were persons of remarkable sobriety—as were *all* Americans before that date—and who, either, now drink quite lamentably as a protest against that measure or who from drinking as a protest, in a spirit of defiance, have acquired the dreadful habit. And this is most marked amongst younger women and quite young girls. It is lamentable; it is horrible, to me to go to the houses of quite nice people and to see a young girl of seventeen or eighteen fall flat, dead drunk on the floor. *What* sort of children will that child have? ... And yet I would not like to say how many times I have seen that happen in the last few years. In Europe and in America! In my own house, too, for the matter of that, and, in that case certainly not as a result of liquor there consumed. ... And always as a Protest. ... And always without any protest against that Protest!

At any rate that was the first time that I had met a Prohibitionist, so I **was** naturally anxious to hear from her own lips the reason for her faith. I therefore asked her pointblank what was her main argument in favor of the measure that according to herself she had most at heart.

She answered that it was furnished by the working-class father of a family who ruined his family through drink, beat his children, murdered his wife and so on.

I said that I supposed that her work on a religious organization had given her a great experience of such cases. She said, no, her work was neither charitable, nor, except in its religious aspects, in any way social. She knew equally no members of the poorer classes whose families had suffered at the hands of drink-addicted male heads.

I asked her what proportion of working-class homes throughout the United States had been broken up or suffered by drunken heads of families. She said she had not studied the statistics; she was now just going to, having had previously no time. The proportion, however, had been very considerable—before Prohibition. She knew it from statements made by preachers and by distinguished Prohibitionists.

I asked her whether any of her intimate friends or any members of her family had ever suffered from the vicarious effects of drunkards. She said that she would not be likely to know people who knew people who drank and that her family had drunk nothing but water from the days of the Landing.

I asked her what proportion of working-class, pre-Prohibition drinking had been indulged in by men and women respectively. She remarked with heat that only a foreigner could imagine that any American woman ever drank.... And then she added almost agonizedly, wringing her hands together:

"Oh, if you only *knew* how terrible is the fate of a working-class family when the father drinks you would not speak as you do against Prohibition."

I said that far from speaking against Prohibition I was trying to discover what were the chief arguments in its favor. But she said:

"No, no. You English hate us Americans.... You want to see us again reduced to your own sodden condition...." And then her whole face became transfused as at a beatific vision. She might have been Joan of Arc—and indeed at the moment she was beautiful.

"And oh," she said, "in two or three years we shall have forced Prohibition on your own country. That will be the great triumph of America.... Her ewe lamb!"

Well, it is pleasant to contemplate the fifteenth-century English at the feet of Joan

REGIONS CÆSAR NEVER KNEW ... 247

of Arc. . . . But whether it would be so pleasant so to contemplate oneself I do not know.

And, for one moment, looking at that radiant Bostonian I remembered one questioning minute I once had in the headquarters of the Women's Social and Political Union Headquarters when Miss Christabel Pankhurst, radiant with her great idea, was telling me something. . . . I thought suddenly:

"Supposing that when Women have the vote they should choose to enforce their views with the devices of Inquisitors!" And I imagined Miss Pankhurst dressed as Torquemada, quietly and seriously holding a red hot poker on my nose until I agreed to some proposition or other of hers. . . .

Well, in front of the Boston lady of the eggs I felt much the same uneasy sensation. . . . You see, she did not know a great deal about Drink . . . but she was perfectly ready, a new Joan of Arc, to invade Great Britain in support of its abolition by law.

Now she was charming if fanatic and, in spite of her years, young with a girlish enthusiasm. . . . And I have yet to meet the American lady who is not. . . . But, hastening over those immense plains, I remembered with misgiving the description given by my depressed New York friend of what he called the real rulers of America—the one or two billionaires and the several million ram-faced, silver-haired, pince-nez'd females who rule the small towns spread over this vast expanse.

And it is difficult for a European to realize how vast the expanses are. If I want to go from Paris to London it is an easy affair. I just do it. There are the hour or so to the coast. You stretch your legs on the quay. Then, shortly you are at Victoria. Or to go from Paris to Marseilles is a small affair. Or from Ostend to Vienna.

But to go from anywhere to anywhere in America is a great affair. You must pack for the journey itself as for a country house visit. Pullman cars are no doubt as good as they can be, but they do cramp your style and their heated air causes martyrdoms or if the darky in charge chooses to leave the steam-heat turned off you freeze. And that lasts long . . . long.

So one travels only after prayer and preparation. I can go cheerfully from London to Birmingham for lunch and be back in time to dress for dinner. But I shall never forget proposing once to some one from what then seemed the next city to New York to go and see him for the week-end. He said it would take three days to get to his city and three to get back—with half a day's wait at a junction thrown in.

These things the European does not realize. On the other hand, the American really feels that if in England he took a too hasty step he would be in the sea. But he should not let his women take that into their sober calculations when they contemplate forcible conversions of the British Empire any more than the European should imagine that America with her enormous distances and divergences of interests can be summed up by the contemplation of any one city or city-type.

Unfortunately isolation and the occupying of situations of local eminence are apt to produce unreasonablenesses. The populations of New York and Great Britain amount to more than the population of Beacon Hill even if you add to it the population of the Middle West. It is forty million against fifty-nine or so. Or if you add the population of the British Empire the disproportion is even greater. Yet not only did I have to hear that Boston lady seriously threaten my country and myself with coercive conversion by unspecified means to a form of virtue for which we are probably unprepared but, in a small town in the State of Illinois, I was seriously informed by a prominent member of the local ladies' club that the Middle West would send armed forces—nothing less!—against, in the first place, New York, and then the British Empire if those two populations did not conform to the frame of mind of her ladies' club.

I was seriously and minatorily given that message by an elderly and authoritative lady in front of a half-circle of feminine supporters. The pronouncement was of no importance, but I sometimes think that if all persons who made similarly gross *bévues* of an international kind could be held up to public ridicule it would be a good thing. For supposing that I had been a publicist interested in fomenting international misunderstandings I could have made a good deal of mischief out of that lady's attempt to appear glorious in the eyes of her subordinates.

Of course similar imbecilities can be paralleled in any country in the world. The Zulus are a boastful race; so are the Dyak head hunters. I once heard a drunken fisherman in Selsey, Sussex, Eng., declare that if the German navy appeared off Selsey he would sink them all with his two-man coble; and the remarks of the quieter inhabitants of a Mediterranean seaport with which I am acquainted when the men of the U. S. S. *Pittsburgh* have been more than usually demonstrative in their unfortunate streets are almost as bellicose as those of any lady in any Middle Western town at any time. Small isolated communities dominated by determined females of a certain age must be censorious and must pride themselves on their virtues. I daresay if the cathedral cities of England and the priests' housekeepers and sub-prefects' wives of France dominated their national businesses England and France would be less satisfactory affairs than they are. And when for a long time a propaganda of what is called uplift has been carried on in a place—or in a wide region—it will have its effect on the moral aspect and agreeableness of that place or that region. That place or region will regard all others as sink-holes of iniquity. I once heard a cottage woman in almost the smallest place in the county of Kent say: "Sussex is the sink-hole of England and Rye Town is the sink-hole of Sussex," she herself having had a numerous illegitimate family by a traveling tinker, her husband being disabled. . . . Well, in the Middle West I have heard it said that New York State is the sink-hole of North America and New York City the sink-hole of its

State. . . . I have heard that said. I daresay the speakers were more technically virtuous, too, than poor old Mary Walker of Bonnington, who is dead many years now, God rest her soul. . . .

And as for Europe . . . God bless *my* soul . . . I shall never forget being asked by a soft-voiced, extremely erudite nun somewhere in Indianapolis if the English were all as wicked as she had been taught to believe. It was in the same village that the policeman knocked at my door long after midnight to assure me that he hated me because I was English. . . . You do not believe that these things happen; yet they do.

Why, in a much, much larger place a distinguished legal character told me that he did not like his wife to be seen talking to me on a public platform—because I was English, but still more because I came from New York. That had nothing to do with my personal record because he consoled me by saying that he did not mind how many times I had tea with the lady in private. But if she were seen talking with any Englishman and particularly with one in any way associated with New York he would lose votes and his judgeship. . . . It

REGIONS CÆSAR NEVER KNEW ... 253

must be queer to come before a judge like that.

Nevertheless, those are the only three instances of dislike for Great Britain that I have personally come across from Middle Westerners either in or out of the Middle West and, as I say, I have known a great many. And they are trivial enough unless, as my depressed New York friends tell me, they really represent the frame of mind of the Governing District of the United States. Where you have many men you will have many imbeciles and ill-bred people. Where in addition communities are small, innumerable and isolated the percentage of such beings will tend to become large. They die out as education and the means of communication spread. And I might point out, at the risk of being accused of self-glorification, that I made a speech over the radio in the Middle West, to what was, I was told, a very immense audience. In that speech I said practically—and indeed identically—what I have said in my Advertisement to this book: that all humanity were much of a muchness; that it was time international differences were minimized instead of being accentuated and so on. . . . And subsequently I received an immense body of correspondence from all over the Middle

West all enthusiastically agreeing with what I had said. And I had no dissenting communications.

So I may hope that my New York friends exaggerate. Nevertheless, I have so many times heard in cold, level, good-humored tones—outside New York—that if New York and the other Eastern States that have a majority against Prohibition do not submit to the will of the other States the same measures will be taken against them as were taken sixty years or so ago against other Dissidents. . . . I have heard that so many times that I am really afraid.

Naturally, one goes out to see what one wants to see; still more does one go out to see that which one fears. The most composed of us are defeatists—foreseers of disaster at bottom. And I have not yet got over the shock of hearing—to give an anecdote on the other side of the medal—of hearing a perfectly composed and reasonable born inhabitant of New York State quite seriously say that within a very few years New York and the Eastern Seaboard must in the nature of things secede from the Union. He said that it was unthinkable that a civilized, cultured, white community could go on for much longer living at the beck and call of a barbarous, censorious, half-educated, Hun-Berserker-Dago collection of undigested foreigners and prudes. At hearing that I fair, as the saying is, jumped out of my skin. But I could discern no sign of humor on the face of my interlocutor and he proceeded to counter my rather breathless arguments to the contrary with a series of historical and international propositions that I was not wholly in a position to combat. He said, for instance, that the agricultural Middle West was not only cutting itself more and more adrift from the rest of the industrial and administrative Union but that, as it were off its own bat, the Middle West was beginning to involve the Union in international troubles that were almost impossible of solution. . . . There were all these utterly self-centered foreign farmers, completely careless of what happened to the rest of humanity, determined to dispose of their endless hundreds of thousands of millions of bushels of cereals to the outside world, as ruthlessly determined on access to the sea either by way of the lakes and Canada or by way of the Mississippi—as ruthlessly determined on that as was ever Russia on access to the Mediterranean. They *must* end by attempting the annexation of British North America. Even now the question of the lowering of the level of the great lakes in the interest of Chicago and the Mississippi basin was causing complications with the Canadian Government. Well, it was a canon of Eastern, Far Western and Washington diplomacy that Canada must be left to the British Empire in order to secure British support against an Eastern power. . . . Why was the whole fate of the Union to be jeopardized because Chicago could not dispose of her sewage without deepening the Chicago river and because the wheat and corn farmers wanted cheaper and cheaper transport to Europe? . . . And why, above all, was the civilized East to be lowered to the level of the incult plainlands?

I am bound to say that my friend had large interests in a power station whose operations are being seriously jeopardized by the fall in the level of the lakes and I am equally bound to add that I have been assured by a United States meteorological expert that the lowering of the level of the lakes was purely a matter of weather cycles and had nothing at all to do with the level of the Chicago river. . . . But the contentions of my New York friend I have several times heard echoed round the club districts of Gotham just as I have—but still more often, and much, much, more often proportionately—heard it said in the Middle West that New York and the East must be coerced into conformity. I mean that I have been only a very short time as yet in the neighborhood of the Loop but I have heard coercive sentiments there uttered over and over again.

You may say that all these matters are no affair of mine; and the temptation for me to leave the subject of Prohibition altogether alone has been very great indeed. I am not naturally courageous and I shrink as much as another man from putting my hand—however impartially—into a hornet's nest. But it seemed to me that it would be sheer cowardice to write anything at all about New York and to leave out all mention of what is after all the weightiest problem of the hour—and the most apparently insoluble problem of the future.

I must say again that I take no sides in this matter, still less do I offer any personal solution of the problem. It is obvious that my sympathies are with the Eastern Seaboard rather than with the Middle West as I know it and that I know nothing at all of the Coast—the Pacific Coast. But I have learned from a long apprenticeship to writing to keep my sympathies within bounds when reflecting on and still more when writing about, matters which have two sides to them. I am aware that in that way one runs the risk of pleasing no one. That risk one must take. I think that the reflections of a person with considerable love for one at least of the parties and no dislike for the other—the reflections of a person who has passed a good deal of time on those reflections, must be of *some* value.

I stand—I and my type, we stand—for a certain suavity, a certain good-humor in approach to all problems of international or of personal contacts. And when nations or civilizations have reached a certain age, as a rule, they develop that suavity and good-humor. I find them in New York; I am told that they do not exist in the Middle West. As to that last I have no means of judging. I have come across cases of stupid insularity in that region—but I have come across cases as stupid in Canterbury, in the agricultural districts of France, Belgium, Germany. . . . In Provence even.

There seems to me to be a very sharp cleavage between the Eastern Seaboard and the agricultural Middle West—but it does not seem to me to be any more acute than the eternal cleavage that has always existed between agricultural and civic interests.

The Eastern Seaboard takes its complexion largely from its great harbor towns, and the agricultural frame of mind has there been very largely stamped out with the relative stamping out of agricultural pursuits—by Middle Western competition. That seems to be inevitable. Small farming cannot compete with large. Even the truck farmer owing to his necessary contact with cities is a quite different person from the farmer of the great plains.

I see no reason myself why the farmer of the great plains and his women-folk should insist that the inhabitants of the great cities and ports should have exactly the same psychology and habits as themselves, yet that does happen. . . . But it would seem to me to be better to attempt to enforce moral frames of mind by example than by coercion. Older national organizations have long since given up as impracticable the attempt to make their peoples good by Act of Parliament.

And indeed I would hazard the generalization that the psychologies and habits of the peoples of great cities and ports *must* be different from those of people who carry on physical or physico-administrative activities amongst the winds of vast plains. I who spend hours daily over white paper wracking my brains for words, or my financial relative who spends perhaps longer hours over paper amidst the constant variations of market news *must* have different derivatives from a Swedish farmer who passes his day from sun-up till dusk over fields of wheat. We must have different exercise, distraction, medicines, food, modes of locomotion and mental safety valves. We must or we must die or go mad.

It is in the effort to point this moral as inoffensively as possible that I have devoted so much of this volume to the subject of food. That is a device. I am actually more interested in conversation and the things of the mind than in what goes on in the kitchens of the world. I like, I mean, Provence better than most countries, yet its cookery is far from good. Far, far from good. But regarded symbolically it must be evident to the meanest intelligence that the townsman cannot eat the same food as the Swedish farmer of the plains. If he does he must die. . . . So I have tried to represent the doctor and the diet-specialist as ignoring that rule with disastrous results as in the case of the Boston lady with the two eggs. I will labor the point a little more and then leave it. . . . I happened the other day to ask a New York specialist—

not a medical specialist—why in her opinion a large number of very nice New Yorkers drank so appallingly on occasion and again, why so many of them made such singular combinations in the way of food? ... I had for instance just before been offered guava jelly with lettuce and cream-cheese which I had indeed constantly seen on menus but had never tried. It had struck me as being, to say the least, startling.

She answered that the reason for both singularities was the appalling dullness of life in New York. You drank there to get some fun out of things and you made your tongue, as the saying is, sit up because you must get some kick from somewhere.

Now it had not struck me that life in New York was dull—but I can see that fixed life in a great city can assume an aspect of monotony. Chicago can go into ecstasies over the visit of a hawk just as the East End of London can over that of a Princess.

And, singularly, I had once made rather minute inquiries into medieval cookery—which was diversified enough in all conscience—and had arrived at an almost similar conclusion. Rather barbarous concoctions of Anglo-Saxon origin—like mince-pies and plum puddings and most consumptions simultaneously of violently opposed viands—are all medieval in origin. In t' e thirteenth and fourteenth centuries people delighted in such mixtures as honey, oysters, assafœtida, peacocks' tongues, cods' livers, cloves and apples. . . . And, indeed, what is the herring salad that is so profusely consumed in parts of Chicago but the survival of dishes of that type? . . . Well, the conclusion that I had arrived at was that the Middle Ages consumed those horrors because of the appalling dullness of medieval life.

On the other hand they had no spirits to drink in the Middle Ages—so they went mad.

They murdered, tortured, held black masses, built cathedrals with decorations of obscene gargoyles, devils, the indecently deformed; they died of plagues, leprosies, murrains; wars, civil strife, commotions were their principal employments; when they were past everything else they went on pilgrimages and died in martyrdoms. . . . They were in short mad when they were not bored—and they went mad because they were so bored. So they sent out Columbus.

Thus my thoughts had run parallel with that specialist's words.

But whether life in modern America is so dull, who shall say? . . . I think that, in effect, what my specialist meant was that unless your mind has the support of the processes of pure thought you will either go mad or drink or eat nightmare dishes. . . . All three, very likely! And pure thought needs the contagion of other thinkers besides you; it needs fuel—both vitamins and roughage. . . .

Well, humanity has never yet achieved a society where original thinkers will be as thick on the ground as all that. Theophrastus' description of the market-place of Athens of the day of Pericles does not give one much idea that Athens in the days of Pericles was so singularly high-brow. . . . And I have already said that little old New York was good enough for me—which means that there I can find enough of good conversation to keep me going until I want to go and do some more work in Provence. . . . That is the beginning of a Great Good Place, for Rome itself was not built in a day.

But as far as I can see the design of the denizens of the land round, say, Chesterton, Ind., and of hundred-per-centers in general is to create an American—an AMERICAN —who shall have all the characteristics of the Scandinavian-North-German-Lutheran farmer. There will be about him nothing

of any culture that has come down the ages.
He will have no trace of French or English
wisdoms. And he shall steam-roller out all
the lights of Broadway and by act of Congress render New York virtuous in his own
image. . . . And he will achieve this by the
aid of Irish municipal bosses and the female
presidents of small-town Rotary Clubs.
That is an ambition like another; a peril
like another.

But I do not believe that it need be very
operative. . . . I was asked to write this
book by some one who has a certain right
to ask me to write books. No, I do not
mean any lady, I mean a publisher. He
wanted me to write a book to prove that
AMERICA had assumed in the eyes of the
outside world the position that Prussia had
before the late War.

And America undoubtedly has assumed
that position—in the eyes of Europe. She
looks like the great, bullying, militarist
Thing that Prussia certainly looked like. I
am using the expression "looked like" with
care and attention. Voices do certainly
issue from the immense plains that sound
remarkably like the voice of the ex-King of
Prussia. I was reading this morning on
the cars an article by a Middle Western publicist. . . . It said that the population of

America was annoyed by the way in which Europe talked about the Debt. If Europe did not cease talking about the Debt, then.... What?... That was not stated!... But one seemed to hear the tread of the iron heel and to see glimpses of the flashing of the sword.... The suggestion undoubtedly was that if Europe continued to talk about the Debt—merely, mark, to talk about it, not to repudiate—United States gunboats running up the Seine would take, for the benefit of Chicago, all the treasures of the Louvre.

It was a stupid and unimportant article by, precisely, the President of a Rotary Club of a small town about a hundred miles from Chicago.... But some European might have read it. I am pretty sure that I am the only one that did and I am pretty harmless. But some one more mischievous might have. And that way madness lies. I and more pacific Europeans and all the inhabitants of New York and all the diplomats of Washington might shout ourselves blue in the face over explaining that this was only the insignificant opinion of a small-town savage.... But, in Europe, we are taught to regard the United States as the Great Republic, all of whose citizens are by Divine Right emperors. . . . Emperors should learn to be polite. We are still paying for one who was not.

For myself I have no settled opinion about the Debt. It seems to me that, should the United States exact it to the uttermost farthing, the pleasant people that I know in America will starve. That I should hate. . . . American commerce may also suffer. That finds me unmoved. . . . On the other hand, should the United States excuse the Debt she will not get much gratitude at the date that we have reached. On the other hand, again, it seems unlikely that the United States can collect the Debt by force of arms unless she employed her late Enemy Nations to do it for her. They are the only peoples in the world to be in the position to wage a war. They have repudiated.

The fact is that I know nothing about that matter. There is no human soul who knows anything about it. It is the first time in the history of the world that one nation has set out to bleed white a group of lately allied nations. It has the aspect of an interesting experiment—promoted perhaps by Teuto-Erse-Negro scientists. It would be quite a good thing to forget about.

For myself I take a more hopeful view of

the prospects of our common civilization. It must disappear if any one of the powers now pertaining to it should revive the late Prussian dream of world-domination, but I take a more hopeful view of it precisely because of what I know—I *know!*—of the mental activities of the great plains.

Let us, for the sake of argument, grant that the Middle West is the great danger to humanity. . . . In the day when I was a boy it used to be said that the pendulum of government of the United States swung between the State of Maine and Maryland. To-day it is claimed that it swings from Chicago and that the dominant generation in Chicago is ignorant, intolerant, corrupt and stupid. Well, the present dominant generation may be all that. I do not know.

But as to the Middle Western generation that is coming along—that will inevitably come into power—I have means of knowing. And I am quite certain that nowhere in the world—nowhere at any rate in that part of the world that makes the North Atlantic into a lake is there so great an intellectual curiosity, so great a thirst for knowledge and so great a determination to put that knowledge in employment. I will not enlarge on what are my particular qualifications to know this but I will simply limit myself to saying that it is my real conviction that the artistic output of the United States is the most impressive in the world and that the great proportion of it—the immensely greater proportion—comes from the plains.

That the output of the United States should be large is not astonishing; its population is overwhelmingly greater than that of any other Western Nation interested in the arts; neither has its youth been decimated in numbers and exhausted in its vitality, its interests and its hold on life. Europe has lost a generation; America has not and you cannot miss a beat in the great clock of Time and keep level in the race.

Those are the fortunes of war. The immense material advantage of the United States at the present moment may be for the advantage of humanity or it may not. Time alone can tell. But the enormous intellectual advances that this country has lately everywhere made at the hands of its young render it immensely more likely that those immense material resources may be put to reasonable uses. Then, both in practice and example the world will be immensely the gainer.

To put these generalizations concretely let me for a moment write loosely. I am told constantly—and that is the European image—that the United States, dominated over by the Middle West, is in the hands, politically, of ignorant, corrupt and practically criminal men of a passing generation and of ignorant, corrupt and fanatically cruel women of about the same ages. We are to despair when we think of Dayton, Tennessee, and to despair when we think of Chicago, Ill. I think the picture exaggerated—but were it true down to its minutest line I could personally view the situation with composure. Even to-day Chicago is a place in which one can pursue one's avocations with composure; to-morrow when the young take hold it may be even municipally and politically satisfactory.

It will be; for you cannot rule a population of highly educated and well-instructed young native-born men and women as you can an ignorant one of middle-aged and indifferent Scandinavians, North Germans, Irish, Finns, Negroes and the Bad Hats of the world. God forbid that I should be taken as asserting that that last is a fair adumbration of the case to-day. It is the case as put by more Easterly detractors of this region. For myself I have seen here nothing but what contented me. . . . But then I moved only amongst such people and in such districts as were likely to please me.

I neither saw nor smelt the stockyards—but then I have neither seen nor smelt the *abattoirs* of Paris. I mean that I do not normally visit the slaughterhouses of cities which I visit or in which I dwell; neither do most people.

Well, the train which had run for hours and hours over the plains seemed now to begin to run through miles and miles of frame houses, standing in the snow amongst the trees of boulevards . . . broad, snowy streets. There, towering up over its levels, was Chicago.

A cathedral is what Chicago suggests to me—recurrently and irresistibly! I mean that, whenever I think of that queer, jagged mass rising up amongst its mournful and illimitable plains I see a vaster and more fantastically Gothic Chartres, a more irregular, a more eager Notre Dame de Paris. And she has about her, for me at least, a note of the pathetic. That is a verbal present which will be resented no doubt by the Chicagoan. I hope it will not annoy them because they are nice people and have done me, as we say, very proud. But still she seems to me, that most splendid and self-conscious of cities, to have the pathos that attaches to the very young person full of hopes but beset with enormous responsibilities . . . a very Queen Victoria saying, at the age of eighteen on ascending the throne: "I will be GOOD!"

The denizen of the Loop is apt to be wild with his figures. Seated in the anteroom of the Blackstone which intimately resembles those of the great hotels of our own Midland cities on account of its dimness and agreeable quietness, I was informed by all the ladies and gentlemen that there came to interview me that Chicago was four times as big as London. This must be an exaggeration.

Unless I invent them I am not strong on figures myself, but I can consult a guidebook and I can read advertisements. Now all the newspapers of Chicago have lately published the figures—not of their circulations as is done in London but of the local populations to whom they might be expected to appeal. This they put at forty million and this may be taken as the population of the Middle West. It is unlikely that they err by diminution.

Morever in all the guide books to Chicago the population of the city is given as three million. Not three million two hundred and twenty-two thousand, two hundred and twenty-one as would be the case with other cities. (The population of the Administrative County of London, let us say, at the last census was thirteen million, four hundred and ninety-two thousand, nine hundred and seventy-three; that of postal London—of London to which letters are distributed from the London General Post Office—is seventeen million, six hundred and forty-nine thousand two hundred and seventy-four. On the other hand, I am usually assured in New York that the population of this city is twenty-five and three-quarter millions. But Harper's Magazine of last month quotes figures to prove that London is by two millions larger than New York. The population of London, then, must exceed twenty-seven million. These figures are confusing but easily invented.)

Nevertheless, the guide books to Chicago assert with equanimity that her population numbers three million. But probably even whilst these words were being written these figures were increased by seventy births, decreased by twenty-two deaths, increased by nine thousand two hundred and forty-seven arrivals by road and rail. You may see a railroad advertisement in Chicago asserting that, I think, thirty thousand trains leave or arrive *per diem* in the city of the Loop—so the figures of population are once more decreased by six thousand and seventy-one departures.... How agreeable it is to contemplate these exactitudes! You will say that there is about all this nothing of the pathetic.... Well, there are many kinds of pathos, but the most intimate note of the pathetic that for me was here set vibrating was one that I have already adumbrated towards the end of my last chapter. It was that of one of the young men who interviewed me in the aforesaid anteroom of the Blackstone. He said—and it was true—that he was a poet of some merit and a critic of considerable erudition. Yet he could only make a living —and a very poor living at that—by interviewing me for, let us say, the *Cold Storage Gazette*. It was not the *Cold Storage Gazette,* nor do I know if such a paper exists, but it was a journal that I should have thought just as unlikely to want its representative to interview me. They probably mistook me for some one else of the same surname.

But though I know that this young man was quite a good poet and a very good critic of letters, I do not think that he can have been a very good interviewer, because his interview resolved itself into his telling me all about his own career and his own aspirations and to asking my advice as to whether he should emigrate to London.

I rather strongly advised him to do so. He had enough money to keep himself in London for a year and I was fairly confident that, by the end of that time, he would have his foot in the stirrup as at least a reviewer. But said he rather despondently: "Since the population of Chicago is so much bigger than that of the dwindling British metropolis and since, in the end, the demand for *belles lettres* must depend on population, was it possible that the consumption of reading matter of that description could be sufficient to support its native reviewers, let alone any immigrants?"

Without going into figures I reminded him that the reading horse-power of a populace depends rather on its tastes and culture than on its size and that, though Chicago may well prefer to read the exciting details of the cold-storage trade, the more effete Londoner had a considerable appetite for serious Reviews and for periodicals known to the book-trade as the Heavies. I myself found them irresistibly somniferous. Nevertheless, from time to time and as if by accident, they would print something good and delicate. So I considered that he might chance it.

The thought has since entered my head that perhaps I was perpetrating a treachery towards intellectual Chicago. For intellectual Chicago complains bitterly that, although she raises almost the entire crop of young writers whom the United States presents to the world, none of them remains in that city once he can see his way to making a living elsewhere. Some one indeed explained to me once that the position of Chicago, *vis-à-vis* of New York and, more remotely of Europe, was just that of Dublin beside London and, more remotely, France.

I daresay the parallel is exact enough. The Middle West certainly produces more than its share of the world's young writers; but when they are not in New York they are mostly to be found in Paris. . . .

But that is not for me so much the pathos of Chicago. That is to be found in its eagerness. For this city is like the young puppies to whom you say: "Poor things! Your troubles are all before you!"

It is true that, in the way of troubles, there was once the Fire. But it is said in Chicago that that was of immense advantage, since it inspired the inhabitants of the city with that determined vigor, that rushing tenacity that, they claim, to-day distinguishes them. How that may be I do not know. Whilst I was there the hospitality of Chicago was so overwhelming that I spent my time almost entirely in dining- or in drawing-rooms, hardly ever going off Michigan Avenue. I will therefore take it that the pace of the city of the Loop is much greater than that of her of the Woolworth Building.

Certainly you can get up and down Michigan Avenue faster in a taxi than you can get up or down Fifth Avenue. It is less congested. But you can get up and down Sixth Avenue in New York considerably faster—and Third, Seventh and other Avenues *much* faster!—than you can the Chicago streets that contain the Loop. But then Chicago is proud of that institution, whereas I never heard a New Yorker have a good word for his elevated railways.

It may be true, too, that the business pace of Chicago is faster than that of New York. I did no business there whereas, for my sins and pleasures, I have done plenty between the Battery and Central Park. But the Chicago people say that they work faster, harder and more ruthlessly than the Gothamites and I am content to leave it at that.

I observed on the sidewalks of Chicago, however, far fewer proportionately of the particular, "ruthless" type of face that very much for me distinguishes Madison Square. It is a face, slightly grayish in complexion, showing generally a thin stubble of bright silver beard. It has singular extent of space from nostril to upper lip; deep lines run from each wing of the nose to the lip-corners. The jaw is remarkably prognathous and heavy-jowled as if with the dewlaps of the bloodhound. On the pugnacious snub-nose are perched pertinaciously tilted pince-nez and the whole expression is that of remorselessness. If the possessor is merely looking after a bus he does it with the ferocity of Nero, and with the same ruthlessness he purchases his evening paper, gives a child a cent or cleans his nails. He eats like a pike snapping semi-circular gobbets out of a corpse.

I do not suppose that this truculence of aspect is any proof of truculence of behavior; it is due probably partly to the belief that remorselessness of expression is good for trade and no doubt largely to Irish descent. . . . To me it appeared that there were relatively fewer Irish in Chicago than in New York—but then I saw relatively fewer negroes whereas I am told that there are actually far more. And there would appear to be—though actually I saw little proof of it—an organized anti-British party in this city. Organized hatred of Great Britain, as

I have already pointed out, proceeds mostly from Irish and Germans or from the descendants of Irish and Germans so that the movement such as it is is un-American enough, but it gets support from such hundred-per-centers as are determinedly anti-European and anti-New York—the latter feeling being probably by far the strongest of all. Or perhaps the Irish movement is the strongest.

I have already adumbrated the case of my friend the country policeman, but I am tempted to say a word or so more about him. Being then unable to sleep one night I was sitting in my bedroom playing solitaire when my door which I had left ajar because of the appalling and unmodifiable heat of the room pushed itself ghostily open and there entered from the corridor a rural policeman. This was in a country inn in Indiana. He told me that he had come to tell me that he hated me. He said that his grandfather had been an Irishman and thus he hated me because of the wrongs I had inflicted on Ireland. I asked him what he supposed I had done to the dark Rosaleen but he only repeated several times that he hated me and then faded away along the corridor without answering my questions. Similarly the nuns in the immense convent school not far away were full of the idea that the English were wicked people, principally because of the sorrows of Ireland. I suppose they teach that to their many hundred pupils. That seems a pity.

It is a pity that any one people should be constantly influenced against any other one people—and it is still more a pity that such hatreds should be made a mainspring in party politics because that at once elevates the mere pity to something of a danger to civilization. But indeed any hatred of body to body is a danger to civilization, for these things have a tendency to grow like snowballs and to gather unrelated matter. Thus it would appear that lately the negro vote on a side issue has been added to the Irish and the German and so a solid mass of anti-Ally votes has been accumulated. And more indirect causes contribute. Thus one of the chief newspapers of Chicago entertains a rooted aversion from England, and in consequence from France because it is said the grandfather of the present proprietors detested Matthew Arnold—as if that journal wished to see United States flotillas steam up the Thames in order to burn the last copy of *The Forsaken Merman* beneath the ashes of the British Museum Reading Room. That is no doubt not true—though I can imagine Matthew Arnold irritating Chicago.

So Chicago contains without doubt a number of hatreds, though as I have said I did not personally witness any manifestation of any of them. The one thing that struck me as an emanation from the sense of which it was impossible to escape during almost every conversation was the hatred of New York. Chicago appears to hate Gotham with a vehemence such as Dublin hardly addresses to London. New York is too large to reciprocate the feeling; indeed I have always the impression that New York has never heard even of the Loop. But if New York *had* any corporate sentiment she might well feel alarmed. She has, however, no self-consciousness and Chicago journals may go on advocating the labeling of all New York visitors with distinguishing letters so that the virgin purity of the Middle West may remain unsullied . . . yes, Chicago and the Middle Western press may go on advocating all sorts of measures to be taken against New Yorkers without, as far as I can see, the stirring of an eyelid on the part of any one on the Eastern Seaboard.

Chicago and the Middle West, then, with their population of about forty million—the population of a large European nation—is practically the America that, as I have said, I have always dreaded. I entered it with, say, about the perturbation of one taking for the first time the desperate step of procuring his first *carte d'identité* from a French prefecture of police. That was precisely the quality of my fears. I was frightened of the unknown things that impinge on one's shynesses or one's dignity rather than of any physical dangers. I dislike for instance being treated as a moron on subways if I do not know precisely how many cents to put into coin-boxes. It is largely for that reason that I have always feared the America that is not New York. . . . And it is largely the fault of Americans themselves—a fault of a kind that they share with all people who go abroad. As I must have made plain, except for a short period many years ago, the only Americans I had met were Americans abroad—either in New York or in Europe. And if the Middle Westerners one meets in Paris find it necessary to assume the aspects, voices, accents and behaviors of cowboys crossed with liberal strains of prize-fighters and old-time Bowery toughs, the Americans one meets in New York almost exaggerate those characteristics. The ex-American New Yorker may very well intend that it is only in dreams that he will revisit his particular Hebrides; but to any stranger he will idealize his abandoned home beyond all reason—and he will idealize it in the direction of ferocities. Of he-mannishnesses! He may be the most civilized of human beings in his private tastes and a gentle poet by profession, but it seems to be a national reaction to outside contacts to represent himself as a devil of a fellow come from hell on earth.

That is patriotism—but it is partly what makes the United States dreaded and hated in Europe where there are no wide spaces in which you could even pretend to have ruthlessly roped violent mustangs. And, though no one spoke a harsh word to me during my short sojourn on the plains, I took refuge in Chicago as might a rat fleeing from a terrier in under a flower-pot. Those vast, vast, vast levels were not for me; when I sit in an observation car I like to see something other than an endless perspective of dwindling rails stretch backwards to infinity and I did not feel safe until I had again turned round the Horse-Shoe Bend and I found myself again at Altoona.

Now let me once more emphasize that I am expressing merely a personal preference —and that I am quite aware that it is a personal preference. I hope I am poet enough to be able to understand the glamour that vast skies, vast level expanses of wheat, unending miles of corn, can exercise on the young mind—and long uneventful days and communings with solitude and young games in barns and twilights and stars overhead. And I am more than aware that if this region is the scene of a terrific mental activity it is probably just because of those empty solitudes and those long communings. I would be prepared to admit if you insisted enough on it that the Middle West is the only Europeanly civilized space left on the globe where a man can get alone with himself to think. Only, it is not for me . . . who stand for small, mixed farming amongst old things. *My* youth must provide glamour for me as pie and its concomitants must for the New Englander—so that if I say that I rather shudder at vast stretches of plain as at the thought of enormous wedges of pie it is an indication rather of taste than of moral superiority. So I fled to Chicago as to a sanctuary where there would be at least some small chambers sealed up from the sky.

And even in Chicago I did not feel quite safe; I had still the feeling that the flowerpot might turn over and reveal me to the gaze of a pitiless, ironic and harsh-voiced

Middle Western Deity. Still, there I was in the cathedral with such benefit of clergy as one could have.

Yes, a cathedral, a sanctuary, a holy place. For the eyes of the whole Middle West— of a nation as strongly populated as Great Britain and covering a territory much more vast—all those eighty million eyes are turned daily to this city as those of Moslems the world over turn to Mecca. I know of no other great city of which so much is expected—certainly it is not London or Paris; not Berlin and certainly, certainly not New York. Those cities exist; some of them administer; none of them is regarded as a leader into a land of promise. You feel that amazing centripetal pressure all through those vast plains and all through the cities of those plains. "It is Chicago, Chicago, Chicago," they chant, "that is going to lead us to a glory such as the world has never seen." It is to happen in three days' time; in three months. In three years at the utter outside.

I read in a great Middle Western organ the quite seriously written assertion that to-day New York is still the greatest port of the Union and the financial center of the world. But in three years' time it is to be Chicago that shall be the financial center of the world and her attendant city to the south its greatest port. How exactly New York is to be beggared in so short a while the writer did not specify, but his article was written with such conviction that for a moment I felt a vague concern. My beloved Gotham might really be threatened. But confidence returned. After all it is unlikely that New York will be beggared before she has had a run for her money and no one can ask more than that. And indeed I care, as I must have made plain, nothing about which is the financial center of the world or its greatest port. I imagine that London actually is but that does not render London attractive to me; whereas, whether she is or isn't little old New York remains good enough.

My first, inner impression of the city of the Phœnix was that here was an immense Great Exhibition—uncompleted as are all Great Exhibitions on their opening days. I once happened to see a President of the French Republic being conducted round an Exposition Universelle in such circumstances. The attendant officials took off their top-hats and waved them towards vast, waste spaces as grandly as towards already existing, sparkling palaces of French Arts and French industries. One day there would there arise the Pavilion of the East. And with the eyes of faith they saw.

So it is with Chicago. Lincoln sits, like a Pharaoh, gazing at the Field Museum in the distance over whole Saharas of waste lands; great placards announce that here will be bridges, fountains, parks; terrific skyscrapers tower down over ruined hovels on what is to be the finest Boulevard of the world. . . . It is as unfinished, precisely as a Great Exhibition on opening day. Yet the good Chicagoan sees it all, with the eye of faith, as it will be.

His face lights up, his eyes sparkle when he says: *"Isn't* Chicago the most beautiful city in the world?" and then adds hastily: "At any rate in three years' time it will be!" And certainly Chicago is on the way to becoming a very beautiful new city and certainly she is attractive and interesting to-day where she is new and where her streets are not overshadowed with Loops and things. And with her parks and boulevards she is so spaciously planned that she must be the most far-flung city of the world. . . .

And I like to think of her as being there, the great cathedral of human hopes rising up over the mournful plains, full, full, full

of those restlessly energized human beings
who run for ever up and down the veins of
that living organism like the countless corpuscles of human blood. May the next
three years be good to her boulevards!

L'ENVOI

So that here I sit in the blazing sun in a white square where the trunks of the plane trees are white because planes have a certain chameleon habit of color. And looking back upon what I have written about my Gotham towering aloft so many thousand miles away I do not feel much call to alter anything that there stands. Distance could not add enchantment to that view, for I don't think that much more enchantment could have been expressed. But neither does it detract. New York does not have white sunlight, white housefronts, white plane trunks—nor indeed does it have the Mediterranean just round the corner of the square. On the other hand, it possesses hope.

That is the last thing that here you look for. The light of the sun: yes; composure: perhaps; laughter, tolerance, frugality . . . an eternal *mi-careme*. But what you do not get in New York and what you do get here is . . . disillusionment. Perhaps in America do you do not get that and that is why

L'ENVOI

Europe regards both Gotham and Old Glory with ironic dislike. . . . Prussia, too, was not disillusioned until very lately.

Almost immediately, stuffing this manuscript into my pocket, I shall go in the narrowest streets, to the Rade, an enclosed harbor, an inlet of the waters of the Mediterranean. That, too, they have not got in Gotham. I shall sit over my coffee and my . . . but that, too. . . . In short, I shall bake my skull in the sun and against the diamond background of the moving waters. I shall see Turks, Americans, English, *braves marins*, ladies of the profession, poets, Malay women, naval officers, *souteneurs*, head-waiters, negro troopers in khaki, Corsicans, Levantines, Algerines . . . all strolling with half shut eyes under the blaze of the sun. . . . It might be Bronx Park on an August Sunday if you could get the sea there.

And a lady from Philadelphia with a French poet for husband will be telling me what New York is like. . . . There is no one in this world who will not tell me what New York is like . . . New Zealanders, Whitechapel Jews, French painters, Marseilles Spaniards, Italian artists' models, Viennese law-students, Greek naval officers, Paris cocottes, each and every one who has never been west of the Scillies will tell me what New York is like. So, indeed, will Mr. Mencken.

But I shall sit lazily in the sun and lazily listen to the description of an amazing place from a charming Philadelphia lady who has only been in the United States once in sixteen years—and then before the days of Prohibition. From time to time her husband the French poet will tell me all about the amazing gunmen, the beer-wars, the unbelievable millionaires of Chicago . . . or the sex-morality of the younger generation of Gotham. Of this last I have no means of judging: I know nothing, or I know too much. At any rate I know enough to let myself know that I have not sufficient knowledge to form a judgment. My glass is not big but I drink out of my own glass.

All these people, Philadelphia ladies, New Zealanders, Mr. Mencken, the Paris cocottes . . . all these will tell me of a New York that I have never seen and all leave out the fact that the note of New York as of all the United States of North America is hope. The dean of X—— and the Master of Y—— will tell me that all the inhabitants of the State of Missouri are Yahoos because they do not know the name of the founder of Magdalen College or that the husband of

Princess Elizabeth Marie of England was Prince Frederic Christian of Sonderburg-Sollenhausen-Ullstein. And if I say that they are hoping to get to Heaven by shorter cuts they will look at me down their noses. But in the end that is what distinguishes the New World from the Old. . . . New York believes that the Good Time is not only desirable but to be obtained this side of cloud-cuckoo land. Here we believe that it is not. Nevertheless, we have assimilated jazz—jazz-dancing and jazz-music. Nothing more innocent, frugal and beautiful was ever given to the disillusioned by those full of hope. In the medieval times the most that the poor could hope for was one day to get justice in heaven; to-day they dance inexpensively from the Lizard to the Caucasus. . . . That is the doing of Gotham. Against that you may set all the Puritanisms, crassnesses, wants of artistry, ignorances and presumptions committed by individuals in the United States and chronicled by my friends Messrs Mencken, Pound & Co., by the Master of Y——, the Dean of X—— and the British Poet who smelt the stockyards in the foyer of the Chicago Opera House, and they will not come to a feather's weight in the golden scales of the recording angel.

And, as far as I am concerned, the proof of the pudding is in the eating. I mean that if one contemplative, nervous, irritable European can moon around New York doing and feeling much as he does and feels in the white sunlight beneath the white planes, there is no reason why another should not, and if two why not two hundred thousand, and so on, including a great population of the less heavily handicapped.

I have been thinking again of the city of the Elite that might be set up hereabouts if we took the Best of Paris and the Best of New York and whatever good we could discover in London and founded a city. But, after reflection, I think not, thank you. For there would then be nothing left to hope for. We should miss the canyons, the contacts, the shadows, the clangings, we should miss the pain and the necessity for hope. We should miss Gotham.

NEW YORK, *1st Dec., 1926.*
TOULON, *9th Apr., 1927.*

**DO NOT REMOVE
OR
MUTILATE CARD**

Printed in Dunstable, United Kingdom